TRANSITION MAGICIAN

Strategies for Guiding Young Children in Early Childhood Programs

NOLA LARSON • MARY HENTHORNE
BARBARA PLUM

Redleaf Press

a division of Resources for Child Caring

© 1994 Nola Larson, Mary Henthorne and Barbara Plum

Published by: Redleaf Press
                a division of Resources for Child Caring
                450 N. Syndicate, Suite 5
                St. Paul, MN 55104

Distributed by: Gryphon House
                Mailing Address:
                P.O. Box 207
                Beltsville, MD 20704-0207

ISBN: 0-934140-81-2

Acknowledgments

Special thanks to our families and children, Heidi, Sonja, Christina, and Deborah, who listened to ideas and encouraged our effort.

For friends and early childhood professionals who offered advice and supported our work, especially Nancy Schoh; past and present staff at the Parent Child Center, especially Kim Herman, Becky Banasik, Kay Davis, Linda Raith, and Joann Zigler; the staff of Manitowoc County Head Start and the Head Start of Central Wisconsin; and the Cooperative Educational Service Agency #5 Early Childhood: Exceptional Educational Needs teachers.

For review of content:

Barbara Wolfe, Ph.D., Early Childhood-Special Education Project Coordinator, Graduate Faculty, University of Wisconsin-Eau Claire.

Ruth Chvojicek, Early Childhood Teacher, CESA #5.

Connie Brown, trainer, National Center for Family Literacy, and Executive Director, HOPES, Hope through Opportunity in Parent-Child Education and Support.

Joan Ensor Plum and Paul S. Plum, authors, "I Am Special" religious series.

Hilari Hinnant, child care instructor, Madison Area Technical College.

For typing our manuscript, Becki Farrell.

For individual ideas: Nicki Nutter, Shoua Vue, Colleen Hannafin, Gail Mattison, and Debbie Hockerman.

Dedication

To young children and teachers everywhere,
who share the magical experience of learning
and to our husbands, the three J's,
John, Jeff, and Jim,
for their constant encouragement and support.

Contents

Introduction

We strongly believe that as teachers we need skills and strategies to guide young children through daily activities and transitions. A transition is the movement of children between one activity or routine to another. Children are in transition during clean-up, while waiting for group time to begin, or while moving from one place to another. We have based this observation on our personal experiences in working with young children and adults in early childhood programs.

Often, the difference between chaos and order in a preschool classroom is the teacher's ability to anticipate and avoid problem situations (Mitchell, 1982). Our strategy for positive classroom management is called *Triple A: Anticipate, Act, and Avert.* Our ability to use this strategy in the classroom, and avoid chaos, is based on several factors. Teachers of young children must have a sound knowledge of child development along with age-appropriate expectations. They must pay careful attention to the activities they plan and the environment they prepare for children. Finally, by developing an age-appropriate schedule and guiding children through daily transitions, teachers can eliminate many difficult situations.

Wouldn't it be nice if transitions could be mastered by a simple wave of the wand? We know there are no magical answers for difficult situations that we face in our teaching. However, there is something magical about teachers who know how to guide children deftly and smoothly through the day. These teachers have the finesse of a seasoned magician. They set the stage through planning and preparation of the environment and materials. They juggle their acts by designing an age-appropriate schedule to follow. Most importantly, they capture the children's attention when they present engaging, age-appropriate activities that promote smooth transitions.

It is with these elements in mind that we have written this book to assist you through daily transitions. We sincerely hope that our book will give you new skills and ideas that will make transitions a magical time for you and your children.

Some Suggestions on How to Use this Book

We wrote *Transition Magician* to serve as an evaluative process as well as a transition resource book. In part 1, you will examine your classroom environment and schedule. The evaluation tools will help you determine if your environment and schedule are appropriate for children ages three to five years. They will also help you identify problem areas that can add stress during transitions. The ideas in the Resource section will work best if you have used these evaluation tools first.

Over the course of three years, one of the authors developed these tools for use in in-services. Their content is based on developmentally appropriate guidelines and the author's experiences and observations. The tools were field tested in child care centers and Head Start programs. As a result, programs reported that using these tools and guidelines made the day—and especially the transitions—easier and smoother for everyone. Using these tools either singly or with your staff stimulates thinking and provides a springboard for discussion and ideas for change. If needed, staff can develop an action plan for change.

Once your schedule and classroom are prepared, part 2 provides you with tried-and-true transition ideas based on our classroom experiences. In selecting ideas for this book, we chose ones that promote self-control, self-management, and cooperation among children during transitions. We've included ideas for getting children's attention, settling children, extending activities, making valuable use of wait time, and promoting constructive child-to-child interactions.

To benefit the most from this book, start with the evaluation process in part 1. This is the *anticipate* part of your new Triple A teaching strategy. Next, *act*, using the action plan for change and, finally, try the new ideas found in part 2 to *avert* problem situations.

"The evaluation was an eye-opener to me the first time I did it. I have done it numerous times since, whenever my schedule needs adjusting, and it helps every time."

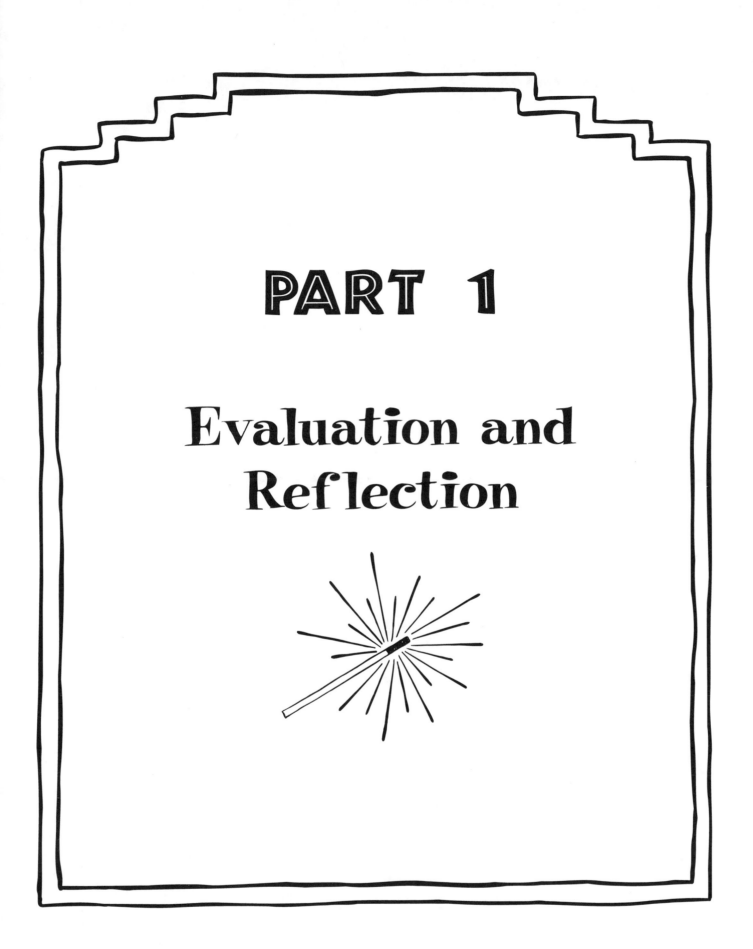

PART 1

Evaluation and Reflection

The Magician's Routine

Children were moving from free play to group time. One hundred and fifty pieces from five thirty-piece puzzles were strewn across the floor. The teacher was helping two children sort out the puzzles. The teacher's assistant was sweeping up sand that a child had dumped on the floor five minutes after the children were told to clean up. Two children were feeding the fish. Several children were in the group area. One was taking over the missing teacher's role by shouting, "Sit down, get ready, do you need a time out?" When no one responded, she made a direct beeline to the teacher to tattle. Fifteen minutes later, the teacher finally made it over to group time while mumbling under her breath, "One transition down, and seven more to go...."

Do you see yourself or your staff in this transition scenario? What problems were created? How can you change the scene to make a smoother transition? Would you like a new way of looking at your environment, schedule, and transitions?

Below are three areas of classroom management to evaluate and examine in order to avert the chaotic transition described above. Use these guidelines as themes for training staff.

1. Set the stage for learning and order.

2. Juggle your day (schedule) for balance and age-appropriateness.

3. Smooth the way for easier transitions.

Setting the Stage

Reducing behavior problems requires looking at all aspects of classroom management: room arrangement, schedule, and transitions. In the scenario above, the environment, the materials the children used, and the staff's management of the transition all contributed to the chaos.

An orderly environment creates calmness and reassures children. Just as a magician prepares a stage and readies the props for her magic act, prepare the classroom for learning. Take time to arrange your classroom and prepare materials each day before the children set foot into the room.

Children benefit from a prepared environment for several reasons. First, an organized and accessible environment eases daily transitions, promotes children's independence, and provides opportunities for learning and decision making. Children can get toys and materials and put them away without your help. They can move around the room easily because pathways and play areas are well marked. They do not have to wait for others, something that often triggers misbehavior.

Second, a prepared environment reduces the opportunities for conflict. In a carefully prepared setting, children interact with other children in constructive, developmentally appropriate activities and learning centers.

Third, prior planning and preparation allows you to devote more time and attention to each child as they enter the classroom. This initial contact time is invaluable in building rapport as well as a time to guide them into the environment.

Often, your facility or room arrangement contributes to your transition woes. How does *your* classroom environment ease or stymie daily transitions?

Evaluation

We have provided you and your staff with the classroom evaluation scale. This checklist will help you identify the sources of potential problem areas created by environmental arrangements and planning. Take a few minutes to evaluate your classroom using the scale and the questions that follow. You may photocopy these pages for yourself and your staff.

Classroom Evaluation Scale

DIRECTIONS: Using a scale of 1 to 5, rate your classroom by circling the appropriate number. Circle 2 or 4 if you think your classroom falls in between the stated criteria.

Selecting Materials

1	2	3	4	5

An insufficient amount of toys and equipment per child. Or all toys and equipment owned by the center are out. Materials are not rotated. Many broken or incomplete toy sets.

A sufficient number of toys are provided, but children have a limited variety of choices. Occasionally, a new toy or piece of equipment is added.

An option-filled environment is provided. Activities and materials are selected based on the children's needs and interests. A range of developmental play choices are provided each day. Activities that are of interest are planned. Learning centers provide children opportunities to play alone, with another child, and with several children with the teacher's guidance.

Developmental Appropriateness

1	2	3	4	5

Children are either bored or frustrated by the toys and activities because they are too simple or complex. No guidance for selection is provided. Activities are planned at one skill level.

Activities are planned for a range of skills and abilities but not on a consistent basis. Little individualizing of activities is done.

Toys and activities are appropriate for a range of developmental levels. Activities for children with special needs are planned. Teachers guide children to appropriate toys and activities.

Accessibility/Storage

1	2	3	4	5

Children's art supplies and materials are kept in closed cupboards or up high. Teacher assistance is necessary. Toys and materials are placed in one container or box. Toys do not have a specified place on the shelf. Dress-up clothes are stored in a box.

Toys bins are unlabeled. Storage shelves for some toys are accessible to children. Teacher assistance is required for some items such as books, paints, and scissors, which are stored out of reach. Teacher materials are generally out of sight and reach.

The majority of materials and equipment are accessible to the children (the room is "child friendly"). Materials are stored on low open shelves, toys and materials have a place and containers and shelves are coded so children can get and return them. Accessible personal space is provided for children's belongings, identified with the child's name. Teacher storage is clearly defined for children.

© 1994 *Transition Magician*, Redleaf Press, 450 North Syndicate, Suite 5, St. Paul, MN 55104, 1-800-423-8309

Room Arrangement

1	2	3	4	5

1		3		5
Arrangement of the room creates congested pathways; traffic patterns cut through play areas or create open space that invites running.		The room has identified learning centers but little attention has been paid to balancing active and quiet play areas. Pathways are narrowly defined and children can't see from one play area to another. (Confined.)		Equipment and interest centers are arranged so children can move easily from one area to another. Individual and quiet activities are placed together and away from traffic flow. Noisy, active centers are placed close to each other. There is a balance of active and quiet activities.

Large Group Area

1	2	3	4	5

1		3		5
The large group space is surrounded by toy and book shelves. Children look out at the full classroom or toward the doorway. Little or no thought is given to sitting surfaces for children.		Group time focus in toward the teacher or situated in a corner of the room. Some care is taken to drape open shelves on either side of the group area.		Group time space is placed out of the flow of traffic. Group time space is situated away from toy/book shelves. A carpet or individual sitting places define the group area. The teacher brings to the group area only the things she expects children to focus on plus materials for wait time.

Play Spaces

1	2	3	4	5

1		3		5
Learning centers are not clearly defined. Children don't have a sense of being in a certain center. Centers are often crowded. Children seem disoriented or confused and sometimes aggressive as a result of the crowding.		Limited number of learning centers are provided. Any number of children can play in a given space or teacher closely regulates number of children in centers. Boundaries are not always clear. No space to be alone.		Spaces are provided where the entire class can gather, or where children can play in groups of two to four children. A space where children can retreat or be alone is provided. Ample space is provided in learning centers such as the block and dramatic play area. The room is organized in clearly defined areas. Each area is pictorially labeled. Low dividers, shelves, pieces of carpet define areas. Children can self-regulate movement between play areas.

Supervision

1	2	3	4	5

1		3		5
Some play areas are not visible to teachers. Teachers congregate in one area leaving other parts of the room unsupervised.		Teachers are present to oversee activities, but seldom get directly involved. Staff occasionally scan the room.		Equipment and furniture are arranged so that children are easily observed. Low shelves or dividers are used. Teachers move about the room as children play and are available to observe and guide. Teachers have awareness of where children are in the room.

After completing the rating scale, take each point and ask yourself:

★ 1

Do I provide an option-filled environment?   YES   NO

Do I know children's interests?   YES   NO   SOMETIMES

Do I provide thoughtful play choices based on children's current interests?   YES   NO   SOMETIMES

For example, if children are interested in writing, do I provide a
writing table with pencils, paper, envelopes, stencils, etc.?

What changes could I make?

_____

_____

_____

★ 2

Each day, do children have opportunities to play alone?   YES   NO

With one or two others?   YES   NO

In a large group?   YES   NO

_____

_____

_____

★ 3

Do I consider children's developmental needs (social, emotional,
cognitive, and physical) when I prepare the environment?   YES   NO   SOMETIMES

Write examples here.

_____

_____

_____

★ 4

Do I provide manipulatives such as puzzles for all skill levels, i.e., knobbed,
four-piece puzzles to fifteen-piece puzzles for more skilled children?   YES   NO

Write other examples here.

_____

_____

_____

★ 5

Do I plan activities that I can adapt for the lowest functioning
child to the highest functioning child?   YES   NO

Write some examples here.

_____

_____

_____

© 1994 *Transition Magician*, Redleaf Press, 450 North Syndicate, Suite 5, St. Paul, MN 55104, 1-800-423-8309

6 In my classroom, do I promote a child's self-esteem by providing activities in which the child will experience success several times each day? YES NO SOMETIMES

Do my activities respect children's growing independence? YES NO SOMETIMES

Write some examples here.

_____

_____

_____

7 Do I encourage independence during choice time and routine times? YES NO

Can children get materials out and return them properly to shelves without my assistance? YES NO

Write your own examples of encouraging independence here.

How could I improve on this?

_____

_____

_____

8 Is my classroom arranged so children can move easily from one learning center to another? YES NO

Are learning centers clearly defined? YES NO

How can I improve this?

_____

_____

_____

9 Do I move about the room observing children as they play? YES NO SOMETIMES

Do I cover unattended parts of the room when my teaching partner is involved with the other children? YES NO

If necessary, do I guide children's play or become actively involved? YES NO SOMETIMES

_____

_____

_____

10 Does my group time area have clearly defined and comfortable seating for children? YES NO

Is my group area free of child distractors? YES NO

How might I change it to help children focus better?

_____

_____

_____

Reflection

After you have completed the classroom evaluation scale and answered the questions, reflect on the following question: "What changes can I make to improve the stage I set for learning?" If you work with other staff in the same classroom, brainstorm changes you can make to improve your environment. Use the quality indicators under number 5 on the right side of the scale as guidance for improving your environment.

In 1987, the National Association for the Education of Young Children (NAEYC) published *Developmentally Appropriate Practice in Early Childhood Programs Serving Children from Birth through Age 8*. One of these practices states, "Teachers prepare the environment for children to learn through active exploration and interaction with adults, other children, and materials." (Bredekamp, 1987, p. 54) This preparation is of prime importance in guiding children's behavior.

After you have completed the classroom evaluation, make a plan to change your learning environment if needed. Use the form titled, "My Plan of Action," found in appendix D, page 123. An optional activity that you can use personally or for in-service and to pinpoint trouble spots in your classroom is the form on page 119 in appendix D titled, "Room Arrangement Observation."

Initially, the planning and preparation of your environment will take time and effort. Eventually, this planning will provide you with more time to interact with the children. When you are satisfied with the stage you've set, you are ready to move to the next step of evaluating your schedule.

Juggling Your Day

A magician's success in doing a magic trick or creating an illusion has almost everything to do with timing. If the magician's timing is off, you will see the card come out of her sleeve or see the coin come from behind her ear. A magician is constantly alert and anticipating. This planning creates a smooth, professional show.

You, too, need to plan a schedule that provides a smooth flow of activities. When planned correctly, a schedule meets children's needs and offers security and consistency. Children need a balance of active and quiet activities throughout the day. It is also appropriate for them to spend some time in large group, small group, and by themselves. An appropriate schedule will include child-initiated and teacher-directed activities. When planned correctly, schedules help maintain order by providing clear expectations for children. Young children will function better with a schedule that pays close attention to their needs.

Without realizing it, your daily schedule may be a contributing factor in children's misbehavior. Often we inherit the classroom schedule from the previous teacher. We might not question if it's appropriate for this year's group of children. We may not take into consideration a particular group's composition or general temperament. Is the schedule you use in the spring the same one you use in the fall? During the year, do you adjust the length of activities based on children's growing attention spans?

These are only a few of the variables that we must consider when planning our schedules. Schedules need to be flexible and adjusted on a daily and monthly basis as children grow, develop, and change.

Evaluation

Determine if your schedule is developmentally appropriate. Use the appropriate expectations evaluation that follows. After you have completed the evaluation, read the reflection section below.

Appropriate Expectations Evaluation

Total the minutes the children spend in each of the following activities during your morning from opening to noon. (Later, evaluate your afternoon schedule as well.) Photocopy this page to use for evaluation purposes.

1. Small Group Activities   _____

2. Free Choice/Individual Play   _____

3. Outdoor/Large Motor Activities   _____

4. Large Group Activities (not including routines)   _____

5. Routines (hand washing, eating, etc.)   _____

Total 1, 2, and 3   _____

Total 4 and 5   _____

Total minutes   _____

Add up the amount of time children spend in:

Teacher-directed activities (including routines if they are

teacher assisted)   _____

Child-choice activities (including routines done independently)   _____

Total minutes   _____

Reflection

According to NAEYC's *Developmentally Appropriate Practice* publication, it is inappropriate to use "large group, teacher-directed instruction…most of the time." "Children are expected to be physically and mentally active. Children [will] choose from among activities the teacher has set up or the children spontaneously initiate." (Bredekamp, 1987, p. 54)

Does your schedule follow this standard? Compare the total amount of time children are in small group activities, free choice (individual) play, and outdoor/large motor activities (numbers 1, 2, and 3), to the total time they spend in large group and routine activities such as mass toileting, toothbrushing, and dressing (numbers 4 and 5).

Do children spend long periods of time in teacher-directed activities? Is the amount of time spent in individual or informal small groups more or at least equal to the time spent in large groups? Does your schedule follow developmentally appropriate practice guidelines?

NAEYC's position statement also addresses the amount of time spent in teacher-directed and child-directed activities. It states that it is inappropriate for three, four, and five year olds to be engaged in highly structured, teacher-directed lessons "exclusively" or for "inappropriately long periods of time." (Bredekamp, 1987, p. 54) Shorter teacher-directed activities and longer blocks of child directed/selected activities are more in keeping with NAEYC's guidelines. How does your schedule measure up?

We suggest a shift to more child choice time and away from teacher controlled and directed scheduling. How much child choice time you include will depend on, among other things, the children's developmental needs, their developmental ages, and the time of the year. Age-appropriate scheduling needs to happen in a well-prepared preschool classroom where there are many appropriate activities. Provide opportunities for associative and cooperative play in small groups of three to four children and individual play time for all developmental levels. Limit large group times to ten to twenty minutes and then only if children are actively involved.

Do you need to change your schedule to make it more appropriate for the preschool children in your classroom at the present time? If your answer is yes, write a plan to change your schedule. Use the form "My Plan of Action," found in appendix D, page 123, to help you put your plan on paper. If you need more help to identify the trouble spots in your daily schedule, use the form on page 121 in appendix D titled, "My Daily Schedule Observation."

Now let's take a closer look at those critical but often dreaded transition times. It is often during transitions that children become frustrated and out of control and we lose children's cooperation.

Creating the Illusion (Smoothing the Way)

The hardest times for many teachers and children are transition times…the times when children move from one activity or routine to another. During transitions, children may be less directed, confused, and/or simply act inappropriately. Often transitions are overwhelming to teachers, too. You may have too much to do and feel frustrated because the transition does not go smoothly. For many, this is not a productive, happy time. Transitions do not have to be this way. Transitions, we believe, can be very productive, almost magical times for children. Prepared teachers can ease children through transitions to the next activity.

Evaluation

Examine your daily schedule to determine which transition times are the most difficult for you. Identify those chaotic or difficult transitions by simple observation. Use the following ideas to help you evaluate your transition times.

Transition Observation

Step One: Look at your present schedule and count the number of transitions in your day.

My total is _____.

Step Two: List difficult transition times for you and the children.

_____

_____

_____

_____

_____

Step Three: Count the minutes children have to wait.

In the morning _____

In the afternoon _____

Look at your schedule and estimate the time children must wait during each transition. Start timing at the end of one activity and continue until a new activity begins. (This counting does not have to be exact, only an estimate.)

For example, in one program there are no toileting facilities in the room and the children must walk down the hall to toilet. Children have ten minutes to complete the routine. Most children will have to wait for other children at least six minutes of the ten minutes.

Reflection

There are no rules about what is an acceptable amount of wait time. However, common sense tells us that the longer and more often children wait during the day, the more likely they will become restless and misbehave. Waiting is not easy. Children are naturally energetic. They like to move, touch, see, hear, and participate in their environment. How do you think they feel when they have to wait? What is it like for you to wait in traffic, in line at the grocery store, or in the doctor's office? Adults often experience similar feelings of restlessness and impatience that children do when they are waiting.

Being actively engaged during routines, including transitions, eliminates wasted time and provides an opportunity for learning. This idea is supported by research which indicates that actively engaging students in learning across activities contributes strongly to their achievement (Stallings, 1980; Hawley and Rosenholtz, 1984). How do you cope with those times? More importantly, how do you assist children in getting through those waiting times?

If your schedule has many transitions, try to reduce the number. Combine activities or rearrange the sequence. In one classroom of three year olds, the staff was sensitive to the numerous times children changed activities. In the morning, children came in at different times between 6 a.m. and breakfast at 8 a.m. During this time, they engaged in a variety of play activities. For breakfast, the staff didn't ask them to clean up. They left their toys, ate breakfast, and were allowed a little free choice time after they ate. This eased the change to breakfast and respected some children's needs to play a bit longer.

If the number of minutes children must wait in a day is high, look at how you can reduce the length of those waiting times. Look at your most difficult transitions and determine what changes are needed. The trick is to keep children actively engaged during transitions and wait times.

There are many techniques you can use to make transitions go smoothly. In each of the following chapters, we'll set the stage with a story of a real-life struggle with transition. Then we will list a few guidelines for improving your transitions thus making your schedule more appropriate for preschool children. Finally, we will share specific activity ideas for transitions and those wait times you simply cannot avoid.

Guidelines for Improving Transitions

1. Plan your transition activities each day. Include them in your written lesson plans. They, too, have a beginning, middle, and end like other lessons you develop.

2. Make sure all of your teaching materials and children's materials are ready for the day and accessible to the activity area. For example, for a marble painting activity, prepare the paint, cut the paper, gather the shoe box covers and marbles, and have paint smocks ready. Decide where you will put the completed pictures. Any missing part of this preparation may cause a wait time for the children.

3. Reduce the total number of transitions in your day. One teacher found going outside in winter was the most difficult transition time. During those winter months, children's outdoor play came at the beginning and the end of the day, which eliminated one or two dressing/undressing transitions. Another example is to allow children to leave the snack table when finished and move to the next activity. Eliminate waiting until everyone is finished.

4. Give children warnings before transitions occur. When children are actively playing, they might resist having play disrupted. Give children notice three to five minutes before they have to put the toys away. This shows respectful caring.

5. Give children who take a long time or have difficulty with transitions individual guidance. Give them a five-minute warning versus three for the other children. Model clean-up and physically give them help to get them through the routine change.

6. Give advance publicity for the next activity. Make sure enjoyable activities follow less motivating periods. "After we clean up, we're going to make a delicious snack with peanut butter."

7. Use one-step, two-step, or three-step directions appropriate for the age of the child. The young child or a child with a cognitive or language delay needs fewer directions. A good rule of thumb is one direction for each year (or less). For example, give one to two directions for two year olds; give

three to four directions for four year olds. Even adults have a limit to the number of directions they can follow. Be careful not to talk too much.

8. Touch, physically guide, and speak individually to younger or less mature children and those new to the program, to help them through the transition.

9. If possible, position one staff member at the new area to engage children in the new activity. Do or have something to grab their attention. Motivate them to come.

10. Give children a task if they must wait. Daily routine and transitions are invaluable learning times for children. Children can practice cognitive skills such as counting; or social, language, or eye-hand coordination skills. Encourage cooperation between children. Ask them to work together to set out the lunch, bring in the trikes, or take down the decorations.

11. Avoid moving the whole group from one activity to another when possible. Divide children into smaller groups to move them from one place to another. This cuts down on confusion, distractions, and milling around.

12. Develop a "Bag of Tricks" for those dreaded transition times.

Part 2 will help you develop your own personal bag of tricks. Magically, you can transform dreaded transitions into fun, enjoyable learning opportunities.

In the activities that follow, the materials, "looped fabric" and "hooked fastener fabric" refer to the two components of the fabric called Velcro™.

PART 2

Bag of Tricks

Sensory Cues in Routine Changes

*T*he frazzled teachers at the What's Happening Now? Child Care Center were at their wits' end. They were in their fifth transition of the morning, with children scattered all over the room. Some were in the bathroom, others in the hall, and only two children had made it to the large group area for music. The teachers had asked the children to put their scissors in the box, pick up their scraps, push in their chairs, wash their hands, and sit on the carpet until everyone had finished with clean-up. Few were listening and most were not remembering all those directions! The teachers were seriously considering having outdoor play all day, to avoid these stressful transitions.

What can be done to transition or move children smoothly from one activity to another? What can be done to end the stress and confusion everyone feels during changes in routines and activities? When trying to get the attention of a large group of children, the use of cues is practical. Use simple verbal directions, along with sensory cues, such as signal cards, musical instruments, or puppets, to prompt children's movement to the next activity.

Consider the guidelines below when signaling children that one activity is over and another is about to begin.

Guidelines

1. The teachers at What's Happening Now? need to check their schedule and eliminate any unnecessary transitions. Often, children become scattered and disorganized because there are too many disruptions during the day.

2. Limit the number of directions you give to children. The younger the child is, the fewer the directions. For example, "Get your cup and napkin and sit at the table." Children will remember the first or last direction in a series, but cannot always process what's said in between.

3. Foreshadow children's movement from one activity to another by giving them a warning. A warning is often a verbal prompt, such as "You have three more minutes before clean-up." Sensory cues, auditory or visual, let children know one activity is ending or another one is beginning.

4. Combine verbal directions with other sensory cues, such as visual and auditory. Help children who are young or distractible by physically guiding them through the transition. Use a variety of sensory cues to signal a change in the routine.

Authors' Note: Some people believe that prompting children with a cue is conditioning. However, throughout life it is natural for us to follow cues. If we didn't have alarm clocks, we wouldn't get to work on time. Signs and traffic lights signal us for safety's sake. Likewise, children also need prompts. Use a variety of cues to avoid the conditioning effect and make changing activities more interesting. Let's explore how we can make routine changes using sensory cues.

Activities

Verbal Tricks of the Trade

Materials/Preparation

★ No materials required.

Procedure

Your verbal cues are children's time clocks. It is important to use your voice to get children's attention and guide them through routine changes. Speak clearly and loudly enough so that all children can hear you (no shouting, please). Tell them to stop, look, and listen. Once you have their attention, tell children the past, present, and future. "We have all had a fun time playing this morning and enjoyed the toys in the room. Now it is time to put these toys away and move on to another fun activity (breakfast, outdoor play or group time)." Make positive statements that encourage even the most noncompliant children to feel as if they are an important part of clean-up. For example, chant, "Everyone join the clean-up crew and before you know it we'll be all through."

Reinforce children as they are working and when they have completed tasks. Specifically tell them their appropriate actions. Positive words, thumbs up, or a handshake builds self-esteem. You benefit by having more willing helpers for the next routine change.

Variations

Another form of auditory "magic" for routine changes is to say, "I need some help. I can't remember what we are supposed to be doing now. Can anyone help me?" When the children tell you, thank them. If the children don't know what they should be doing, hopefully other staff will play along with your game and come to the rescue. If you are alone in the room, go into a brief problem-solving technique with the children such as, "Well, let's see, you came on the bus and had free play time. Are any of you hungry? So maybe it's time to have breakfast. What do you think?"

Body Language

Materials/Preparation

★ No materials required.

Procedure

Using a hand gesture, making eye contact, smiling, moving close, or touching a child's shoulder are forms of nonverbal communication. All play a part in making routine changes and guiding children through transitions. Our goal for routine changes is to have children accomplish them as independently as possible. However, we know that some children require more assistance than others to make this change. So how do we assist children with routine changes?

After the auditory or visual cue, ask children to look at you before you explain what will happen next. For most children, it is essential to establish eye contact if they are to follow the cue. Eye contact, a gesture, or a facial expression can nonverbally communicate to the child to move along with the transition. Identify and teach common gestures, such as a beckon to come, finger to the lips for quiet, nodding your head for yes, and hand up for stop. Teach children American Sign Language words, for example:

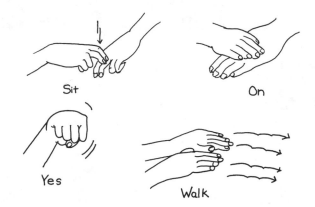

As you give sensory cues for routine change, move in closer to a group of children. This will prompt some to begin the transition. Tactilely guide a child by putting your arm around his shoulders. This makes it easier for some children to accomplish the transition. Also, your participation in the routine change, for example, putting toys on the shelf, provides a model for children to follow. Working with a child to pick up demonstrates a spirit of cooperation. It encourages everyone to move on to the next activity.

Nonverbal communication is also necessary between teaching staff. Convey messages across the room or playground with facial expressions and head and hand gestures. Messages such as, "I need help! Move over to that group of children. Go inside and check on Francisco," can all be conveyed nonverbally. Learn to recognize these universal signals and use them with children and adults in your center as you make routine changes.

Listen to the Bells

Materials/Preparation

★ Jingle bells, school bell, cowbell, etc.

Procedure

Ringing bells is a pleasant way to announce impending routine changes. Be creative! Choosing different bells for different routines makes it easier for children to distinguish the change they are about to make. Ring jingle bells to symbolize music time and a cowbell to signal play time outdoors. Play a chord or a tune on tone bells (similar to a xylophone) to indicate clean-up time or changing from one learning center to another. Ring a soft tinkling bell as children tiptoe to their cots.

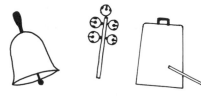

Ring the bell to gently remind the children that one activity is ending and another is about to begin. Always ring the bell at least twice, first giving them a warning to finish up what they are doing and then to signal clean-up time. Remember to include verbal cues with the bells when you introduce new ones. Children need to understand your expectations. One or two directions at a time is ample. As they become familiar with the sound (or sounds), they will usually respond automatically without the necessity of an extensive explanation.

Never use the fire alarm bell (or any bell that sounds similar) as an auditory cue for a routine change. That should have its own distinct sound to alert the children to danger.

Variations

Sing this song as you ring the bell. It's sung to the tune of "Mary Had a Little Lamb."

Ring, ring, ring, ring, ring the bell.

Ring it loud. Ring it clear.

To tell the children in the room,

That clean-up time is here.

Then, as the children finish cleaning have a teacher positioned in the next meeting area (lunch table, group area, etc.) and sing this verse of the song:

Sing, sing, sing, sing, sing with me.

Sing out loud. Sing out clear.

To tell the children in the room,

That lunch time now is here (or near).

Shake, Rattle, and Drum

Materials/Preparation

* Drum, tambourine, triangle, etc.

Procedure

Different instruments set different moods in your environment. Instruments are auditory cues. Play a drum slowly or fast and steady. A tambourine is usually played fast and with intensity. A triangle sounds quiet and tinkly. Play instruments to announce the impending change. Continue playing the instrument as children clean up. As you walk throughout the room tapping your drum, chant positive remarks to the children who are working hard. The more specific you are, the better the children will understand why they are being praised: " (child's name) , I like the way you're cleaning up. You're putting all the blocks away. (child's name) , you clean the books up very nicely."

Use a variety of instruments for different routine changes. As children are walking down the hall to the bathroom, play the triangle to encourage quiet tiptoe feet. As children are moving from free choice to group time, tap the tambourine as you lead them to the sitting area. Play the same instrument for a specific routine change so children associate that sound with a particular transition.

Variations

If you don't have access to rhythm instruments, use kitchen utensils, such as a foil pie tin tapped with a spoon or shakers made of covered margarine tubs with uncooked macaroni inside.

Use other handmade instruments. Appendix B includes directions for making Rhythm Sticks (page 85) and Streamers (page 85). A coffee can with a lid makes a good drum. Cover it with colored or printed contact adhesive paper. Wave streamers to cheer the clean-up crew along.

Tickling the Ivories

Materials/Preparation

* Piano

* Sheet music if you don't know the music from memory.

Procedure

Playing tunes on the piano definitely encourages children to smoothly engage in transitions. To announce a routine change with the piano, play a chord (the C chord is a good one: C-E-G-C) and then tell children the next activity. Also play the complete tune on a piano to make it easy for all to hear and sing the melody.

Play an upbeat song to get children motivated and in the right mood to clean up in a timely manner. Try the following song using a lively beat. (Look for this same tune in later chapters.)

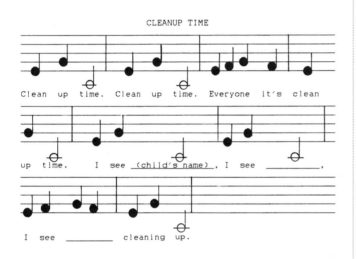

CLEANUP TIME

Clean up time. Clean up time. Everyone it's clean up time. I see (child's name), I see _____, I see _____ cleaning up.

Variations

Another song similar to the one above is to the tune "London Bridge is Falling Down." You can find the notes and melody to this song in a children's songbook.

Everyone, it's clean up time, clean up time, clean up time.

Everyone, it's clean up time. Let's all clean up.

Mooooove It!

Materials/Preparation

★ No materials required.

Optional: Animal sound cylinders, tape recorder and cassette tape of animal sounds, or stuffed animals whose sound is triggered by touch.

Procedure

"Moo," "oink," "quack," and "meow" are all animal sounds preschool children enjoy making and identifying. Associate various transitions with different animal sounds. Make these sounds on your own or use toys or tape recorders to make them. See N' Say toys (animal sound versions) work well and so do animal sound cylinders. The cylinders come in many animal sounds such as a lamb, cow, duck, or horse. A small stuffed animal that makes a sound as you cup it in your hands is especially magical and interesting to the children. To start, give verbal reminders with the animal sounds. Some transition examples are listed below.

★ Moo like a cow to move the children to group time.

★ Have a rooster crow to announce the time to get up from rest.

★ Play a pig sound to transition the children to breakfast, lunch, or snack.

★ Make the sound of a dog to remind the children that it will soon be time to go outside and play.

★ Meow like a cat to indicate the transition to the children's cots.

Soon children will recall the transition simply with the animal sound. Walk around the room or playground making animal sounds or accompany this auditory cue with a visual cue. Turn off the lights and then make or play the sound.

Variations

Music boxes are other auditory cues that give you the same results as animal sound cylinders. Use a music box of a child sleeping to indicate rest time. Find one with an outdoor scene on it to remind children to get ready to go outside. A box with toys on it that plays rousing music for cleaning up the room is another good choice. Decorative music boxes act as both auditory and visual reinforcement for routine changes.

Scents in the Air

Materials/Preparation

★ Items with a natural scent.

Procedure

Sniff, sniff! Have you ever smelled a delicious scent in the air and felt you could almost taste it? Has your nose helped alert you to something that might be a danger? The sense of smell is an effective cue for a change in a child's schedule. Use strong natural scents in your environment that connect with an upcoming activity.

The aroma of freshly baked blueberry muffins signals snack time or lunch. The unpleasant odor of the rabbit cage is a reminder to clean it. Freshly cut flowers or pine boughs in a vase on the table remind children and staff of the need to engage in outdoor play.

We can also assign certain scents as signals for particular activities. One teacher set out cinnamon sticks in a basket when it was time for music. As children smell the aroma, they make their way to the piano and music area. Use floral scented paper or potpourri in a basket to start your science activities. Take care so scented oils do not bother any children with allergies or any pets in the room.

Caution: It is important to teach children to use only their sense of smell with these items—no tasting.

Children respond quickly and instinctively when we allow them to use their powerful olfactory sense to help guide their day. Like science activities that focus on our sense of smell, such as a sniff walk or scent jars, these sensory cues help to heighten the sense of smell.

Variations

Use scratch and sniff stickers or rubber stamp prints, applied with scented ink, to cue children that a particular or special activity is about to take place.

Lights Out

Materials/Preparation

* Electrical wall switch

Procedure

Turn off overhead room lights to signal children that a change in activities or routines is taking place. Combine this cue with a verbal announcement to reinforce the message. Use this sensory cue sparingly, not to condition children, but as a gentle reminder

that a change is coming. In the case of clean-up time, say to the children, "You have three more minutes to finish what you are doing, no new activities. Then clean-up and story time." We show our respect for children by using this warning period and allowing them to complete their task without feeling they have had an abrupt halt to their play. The clean-up procedure allows children to bring their activity to closure, and mentally prepare for a shift in activities.

When the three minutes are up, use a second light cue. Inform the children that it is time to clean up and prepare for the next activity. Say to the children, "Clean-up time has started. Let's all help with this job and then we'll be ready for story time." After you model the correct procedure, allow other individuals to use the switch and make the warning or clean-up announcements.

Variations

If your room has a dimmer switch, use it to slowly cue the group. Leave the lights dimmed while the children clean up as a continuous reminder of the task at hand.

Signal Cards

Materials/Preparations

* Drawings or pictures of daily activities. Mount on poster board (18" x 24") and cover with clear contact paper. Make a pair for each activity.

* Large metal book rings.

Procedure

Help children with visual cues to guide their transitions throughout the day. Prepare signal cards showing the day's activities. Add a word or phrase to the pictorial cue. Instruct the children to look for you as you wear these signs in sandwich board style. Merely walk around the room and signal the next activity in this unique manner. Reinforce the picture

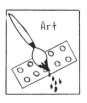

and the written word (or words) as you tell children to view the card for the next activity. A picture of a child dressed in a coat and hat shows the children that outdoor play is next. Say, "It's time for each of you to put on your hats and coats." Another staff person, standing ready in the coat area, helps to facilitate this change in a smooth and orderly manner. A drawing of a paintbrush and paints on one of the cards depicts materials for the art activity on the day's agenda.

The signal cards also work as a way to introduce new activities to the children. Wear and display a signal card with several book jackets and a library card when planning a walk to the library for the year's first library story time.

Be sure to walk throughout the room and display the signal cards where they are easily visible. Encourage the children to get into the habit of guiding themselves as they glance at the cards and anticipate transitions during the day. Have some children create new signal cards as the need arises.

Variations

Display the cards on a table top easel in a particular place in the room. You can find directions for making an easel on page 86.

Puppet Patrol

Materials/Preparation

* Character puppets (purchased or handmade) such as a clown, caterpillar, dog, or chef.

Procedure

Puppets pave the way for smooth transitions throughout the day. The appearance of a distinctive puppet signals children that the time has come for a particular activity. Children develop pleasant associations as they receive a cue from puppets and come to anticipate what happens next. A chef puppet comes out for snack or lunch time. Nancy Neato comes bustling out to let the children know it is time to clean up for the next activity. Other examples include Snuggles the Cat, gently

reminding the children to prepare for rest time; a loudmouthed horse puppet galloping in when it is time for music activities; and Bonnie Bundle-Up, asking boys and girls to dress warmly for outdoor play. As the puppet character appears, one child after another notices the character, and soon the word is out. Ask a child to help by bringing out a character and circulating among the group. The children notice and respond to this friendly sensory cue.

Variations

Use one particular puppet for a period of time. Put different clothes, hats, or props on the puppet to denote various activities, such as a sweater for outside play or a napkin around its neck just before lunch time.

Flip It

Materials/Preparation

* Mount drawings or pictures of two or three daily activities on poster board (15" x 30") and cover with clear contact paper.

* Chart stand with metal rings.

Procedure

It is true; a picture is worth a thousand words. Children quickly grasp the meaning of our messages with a glance at visual images shown to them. Use a flip chart with large pictures of daily activities to show the sequence in the program schedule.

Displaying the pictorial cues in a top to bottom and left to right pattern will insure both horizontal and vertical representation of the day's events. This develops pre-reading skills. The visual representation of snack time, music time, outside play, art activities, bathroom/washing routines, and other interest centers informs children and helps prepare them to move on to the next activity.

Place the chart in a conspicuous place and encourage children to refer to it as needed during the day. The visual cues allow for active participation by the children and help them verbalize what is coming.

For example, direct the children's viewing of the chart as they prepare to go outdoors. Prepare them for choices by depicting the outdoor activities for the day, including the sandbox, tricycles, climbing bars, and sidewalk art. Say, "You have many fun choices outside today. You may play in the sandbox, ride the tricycles, use the climbing bars, or draw with chalk on the sidewalk. Be thinking of what you will do first." Knowing this in advance helps the children quickly make good choices for their activities. Bring the chart outdoors and use it again as the group prepares to enter the building. At this time, the children note that they need to complete the toileting and hand washing routine. After this they go to the carpet area for story time. Children successfully accomplish these tasks and story time begins.

Variations

Mount pictures of daily activities on 4" x 7" cards. Display on a clothesline with clothespins, at the children's eye level. This allows for quick changes on special days when schedule flexibility is necessary.

Step On It!

Materials/Preparations

* Prepare poster board footprints. Cover with clear contact paper. Tape to the floor as desired.

Procedure

Lead children to a particular activity or place in the room with unique footprints. Prepare the special path before children arrive in the morning or while they have been occupied outdoors, on a field trip, or at lunch. Tell the children to follow the surprise footprints to new adventures. It is helpful to station another staff person in the new activities location in order to meet the children and get them started.

Use various patterns or colors for different activities. Some creative ideas include flowers leading to the seed and bulb planting activity at the tables, various dinosaur footprints for a walk to outdoor fun, brown paw prints to follow and find a new pet for the room (guinea pig), or chalk footprints for a nature walk in the outside play area.

Variations

Use a poster board shape relating to the curriculum theme for creating the path. Some examples for these shapes include fall leaves, hats, snowflakes, raindrops, or trucks.

Point the Way

Materials/Preparations

* Pointing Finger Wand (directions on page 90)

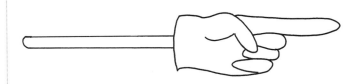

Procedure

This sensory cue relies on the child's sense of touch. Children finish an individual activity and are gently tapped with a Pointing Finger Wand. The outstretched index finger on the wand points them in the direction of the next activity. Encourage the girls and boys to look at the wand, feel the pointed finger, and quickly and quietly make their way to the appropriate area for self-guided play. For example, when children finish their art activity at the table, tap them with the wand and point to the book and puzzle area.

The wand is portable and also works well to transition from outdoor play. In this case, tap children, a few at a time, and point them to the coat area in the building. This process is especially helpful with a large number of children. Simply tap and divide them into more manageable groups. The wand can also keep children on task in a particular area when you are concerned about their choices or safety. Children engaging in outdoor play on a hot, sunny day readily follow the pointed finger to sand or water play under large shade trees.

The pointing finger encourages children to make good choices and allows adults to guide them in a skillful and creative manner.

Variations

Use a piece of yarn around the finger to remind the staff and children of a special upcoming activity. Tape a note to the pointing finger to guide the group.

To Get Started:

Use a variety of sensory cues to signal a change in the routine.

Settlers

Mild Mary and Frantic Fred are trying to get the children of the Whistle Stop Head Start settled into the group area for circle time. Both teachers are helping in clean-up and neither are in the large group area where several children are waiting. Some are arguing about which carpet square they get and Damon has pulled toys and books off nearby shelves. As Mary arrives at the group area, she thinks, "I know if I'd been here earlier, this wouldn't have happened. Some days I hardly have time to turn around let alone take a break!"

It seems as teachers we have so many things to do, especially during transitions. How could Mary and Fred settle (quiet) the children and create a smoother transition after clean-up?

First, Mary and Fred can make a plan to divide their labor so they are in the most strategic places during transitions. Children settle more readily during a transition if one teacher is stationed in the new activity area. Then, even before all the children have arrived, use simple settling ideas to quiet children while others join the group. The following guidelines are helpful in settling children so they are ready for the upcoming activity.

Guidelines

1. Station one teacher in the present activity area and one teacher in the new activity area. For example, Fred could go directly to the group area and individually acknowledge the children as they arrive. Sing a song or do a finger play even though all the children are not there.

2. Ask children to sit on one of the designated seating spaces suggested in this chapter. When children have a specific spot to go to, it eliminates confusion and milling around.

3. Eliminate distractions in your large group area, such as teaching materials that are set down at children's level or nearby books and toys. Drape open shelves if necessary.

4. Positively reinforce children who settle quickly. Children like praise. Praising one child sometimes has a magical effect on other children's behavior. They want your praise and encouragement.

5. Use the following ideas in this chapter to settle, relax, and prepare children for what comes next.

Activities

Places and Spaces

Materials/Preparation

* Blue jean circles (directions on page 90)

Procedure

Having your group area prepared is one key to successful gatherings with children. Prior to group time, place the blue jean circles in a semicircle around the spot in which you will sit. Label circles or place photos of children on them when you want children to sit in certain places. When the children arrive in the group, they can look for their own circle. Talk to the children about the circle being their own space. Tell them that they should keep all their body parts in their space and respect other friends' spaces. This is especially important if you have a group of children who tend to touch and disrupt others sitting close to them.

Variations

If you are not a seamstress, consider alternatives to blue jean circles. Purchase or acquire carpet squares.

Looped carpeting (indoor/outdoor) engages with the hook side of fastener stripping. Place a small piece of the adhesive backed, hooked fastener to the back of name plates or photos and adhere to the carpet square.

Use vinyl or foam rubber place mats in a variety of colors or patterns for sitting spaces.

Save the earth—recycle. Reuse old newspapers. Fold and weave newspaper strips into a mat or fold and stack them to about a 1/2″ thickness and cover both sides with colored contact paper. Then let children individualize these sit-upons with permanent markers.

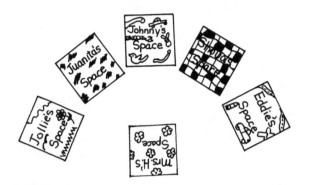

Tape Lines

Materials/Preparation

* Durable colored cloth, vinyl, or electrician's tape

* Apply tape to a floor area in the desired seating pattern. (Test carpeting first.)

Procedure

Guide children to seat themselves for an upcoming activity by using tape line patterns on the floor or carpeting. Prepare and apply the particular seating pattern before children enter the room. Ask them to come to the group time and choose a place to sit on the appropriate tape lines. This freedom of choice, with some direction from the teacher, helps children settle in and quickly prepare for the next activity.

Many activities are enhanced by the seating you plan and provide. Group activities require children to gather and position themselves for that particular activity. For example, alternate the seating pattern so all children are able to see the books and visual aids from their positions on the line. Also, a circle tape

pattern works when showing items related to the curriculum theme or for a circle game.

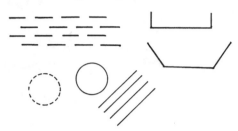

For a special arrangement, tape a design such as a boat or a car. Children are able to sit within this space for the group time. Try special shapes for special days, such as a heart for Valentine's Day. Listening and social skills are enhanced as each child becomes responsible for finding their own space and getting settled. Some days, write the names of the children on the tape lines. This allows them to find their name and place in addition to sitting next to a new friend.

Variations

Tile or carpeted floors have lines or patterns to use for additional seating plans. Yarn lines or Velcro hook fasteners placed on loop carpeting are quick alternatives.

Bearskin Rug

Materials/Preparation

* Create a bearskin-shaped rug made from artificial fur (directions on page 91).

Procedure

Enjoy a bearskin rug as a fun and unusual seating for yourself and children during group activities. Make the bearskin rug large enough to comfortably accommodate you and the children and roomy enough for the group's plans.

Some bear activities include singing "The Bear Went Over the

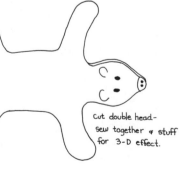

cut double head— sew together & stuff for 3-D effect.

Mountain"; singing and moving to "Teddy Bear, Teddy Bear, Turn Around"; or reading *Brown Bear, Brown Bear*, by Bill Martin, Jr. Children associate these pleasurable experiences with the soft furry gathering space you have provided. Create a variety of bearskins including polar bear, grizzly bear, or brown bear.

Once children quickly come to the bearskin and settle themselves, take them on a "Bear Hunt." This activity excites the children but it also settles them as you wind down the hunt.

Variations

Make skins to look like other animals. Use artificial material with fur designs such as zebra stripes, leopard spots, or lamb's wool. Plan appropriate songs and finger plays to help settle the children.

Blanket and Towel Favorites

Materials/Preparation

* Blanket or towel with a design and colors to match a particular focus, theme, or activity.

Procedure

Motivate children and help to settle them for a group activity by spreading a unique blanket or towel to define the seating or standing area for a small group activity. It is important to limit the group size so all the children fit comfortably on the blanket or towel or use enough blankets or towels to accommodate everyone.

Direct the children to sit on the gathering surface. On some occasions, vary this by asking the children to help you determine where to place the blanket or towel. This allows them to function as a group and make a decision.

Once everyone is seated, ask the children to look at the surface you have chosen and encourage them to think of the topic for discussion or the planned activity. Use a large blue velour towel to create a lake, pond, or ocean atmosphere and lead the children in a round or two of "Row, Row, Row Your Boat" or "Little White Duck." Seat the children on a variety of baby blankets and start a discussion about families. A Humpty Dumpty or Little Miss Muffet design on a towel encourages children to recite favorite nursery

rhymes. Use a brightly colored Navajo blanket to introduce Native American songs and stories.

Variations

Try some other unusual cloths or materials to create the seating atmosphere you desire. For example, use a plant and floral print sheet to indicate a deep, dark jungle. Use artificial turf to indicate a baseball field or park.

Pillow Pleasantries

Materials/Preparation

* Small pillows (directions on page 91)

Procedure

Settle in with a soft, comfortable pillow. Early in the year or as you get new children in your small group, help them make pillows. Encourage children to create a picture of themselves on their pillow. Talk about their pillows and the creative design or pictures they are drawing on them. They might even be able to write their name.

Place the pillows on children's individual spaces prior to group time. As they sit down, ask them to hold their pillow. (What a pleasant and relaxing feeling pillows create!) Talk about individual differences as they come for group time. When all children have arrived, place two baskets in the middle of the circle. Use the pillows to take attendance. Sing a song or make a statement about the children being here today as each comes up and places their pillow in one basket. If some children are gone that day, place their pillow in the other basket. Talk about missing friends who are absent that day.

For children more skilled with numbers, count how many pillows are in each basket. Decide if more children are here, more children are gone, or if the numbers are equal.

Use the pillows for various activities throughout the group time or for resting.

Variations

Pillow babies and matching fabric beds are another soft sculpture object. Directions for making Pillow Babies and Beds are on page 92. When using pillow babies, place the baby on the children's individual spaces. As they come to group, each child chooses a space. Then they find the matching fabric bed for their baby located in the basket in the middle of the group area. Have the children tuck their babies into the matching bed.

Once all the children have arrived and are sitting on their spaces with their babies, and their babies are tucked comfortably in their beds, sing some relaxing songs. Pretend to feed and rock the babies until they are asleep. Then have the children place the pillow babies in the basket and continue your group time.

Just like small pillows, use pillow babies for many different activities throughout the day. Take them for a walk around the block. Children benefit from experiencing how to care for a baby.

Vehicles

Materials/Preparation

* A vehicle, such as a farm wagon or canoe

Procedure

Bring a vehicle into the classroom and create a fun and interesting atmosphere for a small group activity. Direct children to inspect and investigate the vehicle set up in the classroom or outdoor play area. Make sure any item you bring in is safe, free of sharp or ragged edges, and anchored securely in place.

One teacher brought a golf cart to his outdoor play area. It was large enough to hold him and eight children for story time fun. The girls and boys in his group were eager to settle down for the activity in such a fun gathering space.

Some other interesting vehicles include an old-fashioned sleigh, pony cart, and rubber raft. Parents are excellent resource people for unusual vehicles; encourage them to loan vehicles to your program.

In addition to using a vehicle for a small group time, incorporate it into various parts of your daily activities. For example, set a large rubber raft on several blue sheets (river water) next to a dock made from large wooden blocks, and allow the children to use the area for camping dramatic play. Simple props such as canteens, backpacks, campfire pots, and magnetic fishing poles help imaginative and social play,

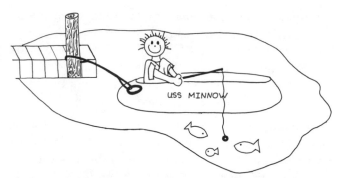

along with language development. The children improve the area by making items such as stars, clouds, plants, or animals to live in the environment you have created. When it is time to sing, read a story, or gather for discussion, ask the children to get on the raft with you. This works especially well when gathering children as they finish individual activities. One by one, they are able to gather with you and get ready for the group time.

Variations

Large appliance boxes make unique gathering spots. Convert these boxes into a space ship, airplane, hot air balloon, or train and use these sites for small group times. (A knife blade on a jigsaw or saber saw works nicely when cutting the cardboard.)

A large parachute suspended from the ceiling makes a circus big top to gather under for group time.

So Soft Sounds

Materials/Preparation

* Music box

Procedure

Soft music is a sure settler. Choose a music box that is visually appealing to the children. One that moves would particularly catch their attention. Turn it on or wind it up as the children come over to group time. Now you have time to greet the children with visual or tactile cues. Providing soothing music truly settles them into a relaxing and productive gathering.

Choose a music box that ties into the theme as a way to focus children's attention on that topic.

Encourage children to bring music boxes from home to add more or renewed interest in this activity.

Variations

Purchase electronic music buttons (about the size of quarters) at craft stores. Put them in tiny decorative felt bags (an apple, bear face, star, etc.; directions on page 93) or tuck one in your pocket. The music buttons play a short tune one or two times through. Then just push the music button again. Pass the music buttons from child to child, giving each a turn to make music.

Kazoo to You

Materials/Preparation

* Kazoo

Procedure

Kazoos are one of the most portable instruments you can find. If you can hum, you can play a kazoo. Pull it out of your bag of tricks as the children gather, and start humming some familiar tunes. Encourage the children to guess the tune and join you with their singing voices. Some tunes that settle children include, "Twinkle, Twinkle Little Star," "The Eency Weency Spider," and "Rock-a-bye Baby." Kazoo and sing until children have gathered for group and are settled.

Variations

In a small group of four year olds, one teacher acquired a number of kazoos, labeled them, and placed them in small bags, one for each child. As the children arrived for group, they found their kazoo and joined in the fun.

End the hum-a-long with a particularly quieting song. Have children return the kazoos to their bags or a basket and put them away before continuing with group time.

Periodically take the wax paper piece out of the kazoos and run the instruments through the dishwasher to sterilize them.

Strumming the Strings

Materials/Preparation

* Autoharp or guitar (strap optional) and pick
* Music booklet and easel (directions on page 93)

Procedure

Autoharps and guitars are versatile and portable instruments. Take one of these instruments with you to group time whether it is indoors or outdoors. Autoharps or guitars are a visual motivator, along with your voice, to get children interested in coming to group. Start a collection of songs that the children know and new ones you want to teach them. Write the words and chords on 5" x 8" index cards and compile them in a booklet. Keep the booklet with your instrument for quick use. As long as your instrument is tuned, it is easy to pick up and play a couple of songs as the children are gathering. The final song should be one that gets them relaxed and ready to begin group.

Continue to add songs to your booklet as children learn them. Draw a picture of the song on the same index card. Now children can make some choices of what they'd like to sing as they page through the booklet.

Variations

In addition to songs in your booklet, compile a list of interesting questions to ask children. General topics to discuss include favorite colors, what they had for breakfast, how they came to school today, and so on. Ask these questions as children are arriving at the group area.

Rolling Along

Materials/Preparation

* Sponge balls, beanbags (directions on page 95), or pom-poms (directions on page 96)

Procedure

This is a good activity to do as the children sit on their individual spaces. Position them in a circle. Have a ball ready in your bag of tricks. A ball works well because it can be rolled. Sponge balls or lightweight bouncing balls are a good size and fairly safe for indoors.

Roll the ball to a child as you sing this song to the tune "Where is Thumbkin?"

Catch the ball, catch the ball.

If you can, if you can.

(child's name) , catch the ball.

(child's name) , catch the ball.

If you can, if you can.

Sing the next verse to retrieve the ball from the child.

Roll the ball, roll the ball.

Back to me, back to me.

(child's name) , roll the ball,

(child's name) , roll the ball.

Back to me, back to me.

Sing the same tune when using pom-poms or beanbags. Substitute the word "ball" with "beanbag" or "pom-pom." In the second verse, use the word "toss" instead of "roll."

Variations

Here is another song to the tune of "Mary Had A Little Lamb."

I toss the bag to (child's name) , (child's name) , (child's name) ,

I toss the bag to (child's name) .

He'll (or She'll) toss it back to me.

Use the same child's name throughout the complete song so they have time to receive and return the item to you. Singing children's names creates magical interest.

I've Got the Rhythm

Materials/Preparation

* Rhythm sticks (directions on page 85), tambourine, drum, bells, triangle, etc.

Procedure

Listen to the beat—again. Purchased or handmade instruments were used in chapter 1 for a routine change. Carry them over to group time and use them as a settling activity. Use any of the instruments listed above to tap out rhythm patterns for chanting. Once you establish a steady beat, it is easy for children to join in. Below is a good individualizing chant to say as they gather. Include last names, too.

Welcome Abigail. I'm glad you're here today.
Welcome John. I'm glad you're here today.
Welcome Suzy. I'm glad you're here today.

Variations

If a rhythm instrument isn't available, clap your hands, or tap your knees or toes. Children's body parts are occupied as they imitate your actions. This alleviates any temptations to disrupt the other children as they settle in for group time.

Welcoming Wands

Materials/Preparation

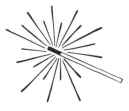

* A wand (a Mylar balloon on a stick or a more detailed sewn one; directions for a felt star wand are on page 87)

Procedure

Wands are magical for children. When the children arrive at group time, welcome them with a wand by tapping heads, hands, or knees for a bit of physical contact. Verbally tell them you are happy they joined your group. Use the wand to greet the group as a whole. Wave it over the group and chant: "Ibbity Bibbity Boo, I'm very glad to see you!"

At times it takes a little more effort to get the children settled. Encourage children to make magic themselves. Tell them as you wave the wand over the group it will get very quiet. Reinforce the group or individuals who were able to magically quiet the room.

Variations

Make a looped fabric circle wand (directions on page 88) that will change with the season or theme. For this wand, you make a circle shape out of looped fabric and add any object, from an apple to a zebra, by placing a piece of hooked fastener on the back. A yellow circle with a smiley face is great fun.

Hello, Hello

Materials/Preparation

* No materials required.

Procedure

Playing music or singing is always a good settler for group time. This song allows children to respond within the tune.

Hello, Hello

Hel - lo, hel - lo, hel - lo and how are you?

I'm fine, I'm fine and I hope that you are too.

Teach children the complete song. When they know it well, sing the first line and have the children sing the second. Reverse roles and have the children ask you how you are.

Variations

Teach children to say hello and communicate in various languages (see appendix C for ways to say "Hello"

in different languages and for Hmong, Spanish, and French phrases). Have parents, co-workers, or friends knowledgeable of other languages interpret the song's words for you. Tape record the interpreter on a cassette as they sing the song in a foreign language. Learn the song in as many different (or more) languages as you have cultures in your group.

Sing the song and do the actions using American Sign Language (see appendix A for resource books).

Breathe Deeply

Materials/Preparation

* No materials required.

Procedure

Help settle or calm children coming from active play to a group time with some deep breathing exercises. Ask them to join you. Take a deep breath, inhale, fill the lungs, and slowly blow the air out (exhale). (Demonstrate this breathing with a balloon.) Repeat the deep breathing three to four times. Ask the children to take a deep breath, inhale, and hold their breath as you all count together, silently, for a count of two (one, two, exhale); three (one, two, three, exhale); five (one, two, three, four, five, exhale); and later ten. Use your fingers to count. Try to hold the air for a longer time and a higher count as you repeat the exercises on other days.

This simple activity will help children with increased lung capacity and clear singing voices, in addition to helping prepare them for the group's activities.

Variations

When children come to the gathering space individually or in small groups, settle them as they arrive. Give each child a small fluffy feather and ask them to take a deep breath, while holding the feather in front of their face. Have them exhale slowly and make the feathers move as they blow.

Tongue and Mouth Twisters

Materials/Preparation

* No materials required.

Procedure

Make good use of time as children gather for a group activity; practice tongue and mouth exercises. Demonstrate and direct children to give their tongues and mouths a good workout. Try these special mouth movements to settle the group and improve articulation skills.

Encourage the children to follow your directions as you say, "Move your tongue from side to side, inside your mouth and then outside your mouth. Move your tongue in and out, slowly and then quickly. Use your tongue to touch your nose, your chin." Ask children to curl up or roll the sides of their tongues. This can be described as making the tongue look like a taco shell. Children love to share this activity with their family members at home. Not everyone is able to roll their tongue. It's hereditary! Acknowledge the endeavors of the children and encourage them to help think of more movements.

Variations

Our mouths are also capable of making many interesting sounds. Ask the children to try some sounds that everyone can do. "Make a sound with your tongue and the roof of your mouth." (Cluck, cluck) "Make some noises as you open and close your mouth in many ways." (Pop, pop, kiss) "Make some sounds that are quiet and then loud." (Peep, meow, grr, boo) Allow the children to offer suggestions for movements and sounds to exercise their tongues and mouths, too.

Reflections

Materials/Preparation

* Large, unbreakable mirror
* Small plexiglass mirror for each child

Procedure

It is important to help children understand the function of a mirror and its unique traits when first presenting this settling activity to them. Of course, most children see mirrors in their everyday life, on cars, in stores, or at home.

Hold up a large mirror and tell the children to look into it as a group. Talk about the word reflection. Ask them to identify people by name as you point to them on the mirror. Then ask them to do a simple action (touch their finger to their nose) and watch as it is happening. Some, who know left from right, notice that the mirror uses the opposite hand when it shows us doing an action. Point this out to the children.

Next, ask one child to stand up and move slowly among the other children. Discuss how this looks in the mirror.

Put aside the large mirror and give each child a small plexiglass mirror. Direct them to make faces, wave, move a body part, or do a motion as they observe themselves in the mirror.

Next, put the mirrors down and tell the children to pretend to be mirrors as you do some movements in front of them. Lead the children in a series of movements, using one body part, a hand or foot, to start. Do this slowly with distinct movements so the children can follow. Continue for about thirty seconds the first time it is presented. Encourage the children to concentrate and follow very closely with their eyes. As you repeat the activity, ask the children to lead the group or have them work in pairs and make reflections of each other. After the children are able to do the activity successfully, move more than one body part.

Variations

Try to imagine the reflections we sometimes see on water or in distorted mirrors. Use a sample and allow the children to improvise. Aluminum foil mounted on poster board creates a passable distorted mirror and will allow the children to use their imagination.

I Stretch My Hands

Materials/Preparation

* No materials required.

Procedure

There are times when children need a final cue to clarify that group time is beginning. Choose a song with actions where the last movement is placing your hands in your lap. This is a short, simple one.

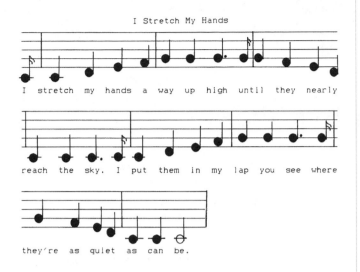

I Stretch My Hands

I stretch my hands a way up high until they nearly reach the sky. I put them in my lap you see where they're as quiet as can be.

Have children seated as you do this settling song. Sing it in a quieting voice. If the first time through doesn't settle the complete group, sing it one or two more times, getting quieter and slower each time.

Remember to reinforce appropriate sitters. "I like the way Nancy and Leah are ready for group." "Look how quickly Vern got settled!"

To Get Started:

Choose calming activities in a designated area to settle children for the upcoming activity.

Attention Grabbers

It was one of those days. Ms. Miriam, the kinder-garten's student teacher, wondered if she would ever learn the secret of how to get the children's attention. At story time, she held up her book and started reading, hoping the children would settle down and stop talking. After several pages, even more children were talking. Why weren't they listening? She put the book down and said, "I'll wait until you are all quiet." She waited and then started the story. They started chatting again. In frustration she said, "Do I have to stand on my head to get you to listen?" Juanita responded, "Oh, yes! Can you really do that?"

Ms. Miriam needs an attention grabber (like standing on her head) to help children move into the story. Children are naturally curious; by presenting a unique object with a little mystery, suspense, or surprise, Ms. Miriam can draw young children into an activity. Once she successfully makes the transition into the next activity, the children are more likely to pay attention to her well-planned lesson.

Below are additional guidelines for using attention grabbers with children.

Guidelines

1. Write attention grabbing transition activities into the introduction portion of your lesson plan. Think of ideas that will create interest and moti-vate children to want to hear more.

2. Make sure all of your teaching materials (includ-ing your attention grabber) and the children's materials are ready for the upcoming activity. Place them close by. You can, without delay, bring out your attention grabber and begin your discus-sion about the new activity.

3. Give advance publicity for the coming activity. "After we clean up, we're going to find out what is in that large sack by my chair." This motivates the children to complete that task at hand. The sack becomes an attention grabber.

4. Settle all the children before you bring out or reveal your motivator.

5. Create an atmosphere of anticipation with your questioning technique. "What do you think I have in this teeny tiny bag?" After they have made some guesses, offer clues. By asking children questions you can create a sense of mystery or surprise.

Activities

Bags, Bags, and More Bags

Materials/Preparation

* An interesting, attractive bag with an object inside. Collect bags of all sizes, colors, designs, and materials (handmade or purchased). Examples: paper, tote, cloth, gift bags, zippered bags.

Procedure

Help children make the transition to your lesson by using bags to introduce your unit's theme, today's book, or your nutrition lesson. Use children's natural curiosity to grab their attention and help them focus on what you've planned.

In one program, the nutrition activity was introduced with a magic bag. The teacher started by asking ques-tions: "What do you think we're going to make today for snack? There is something in this bag that will tell us. What do you think we need if we were going to cook something? Rossi thinks there is a spoon in the magic bag. What else is in the bag?" Questions like these promote critical thinking skills. The magic bag with a prop helps children transition to the planned activity.

Caution: Overuse of your magic bag may cause the novelty to wear off.

Variations

Besides the magic bag, use other bags at different times and for different occasions. A tiny bag might introduce something small. A bag decorated with cats, mice, or rabbits may be a clue itself. For a tactile identification by children, ask them to feel the object from the outside of the bag to help them make their guesses.

BIG Bags

Materials/Preparation

* An adult size cloth bag, about 4' x 6'. Sew your bag from any brightly colored fabric. Make two handles at the top and cut two slits for holes in the bottom for the feet. If you don't sew, use a glue gun.

Procedure

Children love the element of surprise. If it's a big, disguised surprise it's even better. Grab their attention and introduce a guest or a new activity at the same time. Bring your visitor into the classroom in a large bag. A staff person can hold the top closed and help guide that person into the room. Using open-ended questions, ask children, "Who do you think is in our bag today? Is it a boy or a girl? Can we tell from looking at the shoes?" Reveal part of the person's head to give children more clues. Perhaps parts of the guest's costume, such as a clown's brightly colored wig or big ear. Give additional information if they are having difficulty guessing. The suspense usually holds children's attention and helps you move into the upcoming activity.

Variations

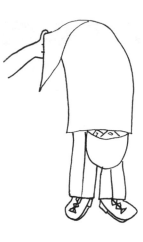

Slip the large bag over the person with the bottom open to allow for walking. As you slowly pull the bag up over the person's body, have the children guess who the special guest is by the clothes they are wearing or items they're holding. For example, invite a mail carrier and ask her to hold a mail bag and letters.

Getting Ready for Guests

Materials/Preparation

* A specific prop that belongs to or would help identify your invited guest.

Procedure

Sprinkle your monthly planning with visits from resource people who represent your week's theme. Help children focus on this invited guest by bringing in a prop that offers some clues to children. Examples: a huge toothbrush for a dentist, a trick leash with invisible dog for a veterinarian, or a loud bicycle horn for a clown. Create suspense and surprise with the prop by asking questions before the guest enters the room. Children love guessing. The prop and the guessing game help children with the transition from the previous activity to the invited guest.

Variations

Another attention grabber is having you or another staff dress up in costume. Dressing as Mother Goose or Anna Aerobics helps children focus their attention so you can move into the planned activity. Mother Goose visits the classroom and reads several books and then leaves. Anna Aerobics comes in to lead exercise time. The clothing or costumes make the new activity attractive to children.

Nesting Objects

Materials/Preparation

* Purchased nested tins or graduated sizes of plastic eggs

* Make your own nesting sets from baskets or bags. Select sizes that fit into each other. Decorate the baskets, if necessary, to make them attractive.

Procedure

Nesting sets are a fascination to preschool children. They are a novel way to grab children's attention, increase suspense as you open one after another, and move them into the next activity. One teacher nested several bags of graduated sizes ending with a teeny tiny bag. She used that teeny tiny bag to start the following story: There was a teeny tiny lady who went shopping with her teeny tiny bag and—(let the children finish the story). This involved the children right away and got their attention focused on the story.

Hide an object such as a small puppet or wind-up toy in the last tin, plastic egg, or basket of a nested set. It always delights children to discover something hidden. It only takes a few minutes to do this, but makes this attention grabbing transition smoother.

Variations

Use purchased nested sets, such as family members, kittens, or dolls. As you show and take apart the set, ask questions to promote critical thinking and problem solving. "What is this? What comes next? Will it be bigger or smaller? Will we come to the end this time?" Reversing the process by putting it back together is also excellent for cognitive skill development.

Place the nesting objects on magic carpet activity shelves (see chapter 6) so children can explore further during wait time.

Get a Clue

Materials/Preparation

* A clue box. Use a box about 12″ x12″ x12″. Cover with colored contact or construction paper and place a special object inside. Prepare up to six clues. Tape each clue to a side of the box, placing the last clue on the top.

Procedure

As children gather, announce and show that you brought a clue box today. Explain what a clue box is the first time you use it. "Today I brought a clue box. This box has something inside that we are going to talk about this week. Clues about what's inside are written on the outside of the box. I will read each clue and see if you can guess what is inside." Choose objects that are theme related and something of interest to the children. For example, a magnifying glass or model dinosaurs. Start by choosing one side of the box and reading the first clue. Continue around the box, doing the lid last. Children will offer guesses as you go. Their natural curiosity will keep their attention to the very end. Praise all the children for their interesting and thoughtful guesses. Now, you and the children are ready to open the box and move to your planned lesson.

Variations

The box you choose can be any size depending on the size of the item. By varying the size you bring in, you will continue to get the children's attention. You can also use two boxes, one inside the other, for added clues that will heighten the anticipation.

Guess Again, If You Can

Materials/Preparation

* Prepare your guessing questions.

Procedure

Older preschoolers enjoy the challenge of solving riddles or little guessing games. Trying to guess the answer or solve the problem surely will grab their attention. The first time you do this with children, explain that a riddle is like trying to solve a problem. Start with something that is familiar to them. For example, if you are starting a new unit on firefighters you could say, "Listen to my questions. Let's see if you can guess what we will be talking about this week. These community helpers wear hard helmets and rubber coats to protect them from falling objects and water. Who are these community helpers?" If they are successful in guessing, provide another set of questions related to the unit. Children's natural curiosity will draw them into the discussion about the new unit. Just remember that the questions need to be appropriate for the child's age and need to relate to children's life experiences.

Variations

Show children a riddle box (directions on page 98). A riddle box has a picture on each side covered with a flap. The riddles could describe what you are talking about for the week's theme, such as pets—cat, dog, bird, fish. One clue could be, "With yarn balls I like to play. Meow is what I say."

Mystery Bulletin Boards

Materials/Preparation

* Prepare a bulletin board with theme-related pictures such as community helpers, pets, animals. Cover each picture with construction paper and tape down.

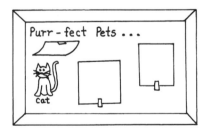

Procedure

Children's curiosity and love of guessing games are sure attention grabbers. At circle time, introduce the new surprise bulletin board. Explain that this surprise bulletin board is about our pets (which might be your theme). "Under each of these papers is a picture of a special pet. It may even be a pet like yours. In order for you to see what is under these papers, you will have to guess." Ask children to name a pet. If they guess one of the pets pictured, reveal the picture. If children run out of guesses, provide clues to help them correctly guess the remaining pets. You may play this guessing game in one sitting or do a few pictures

each day. Continue until all the pictures are uncovered. This activity only takes a few minutes and children are ready to move into the next activity you have prepared.

Variations

Decorate a bulletin board with a character such as a snowman or scarecrow. Make it large so the children can easily see it at group time. Mount the illustrations in pieces (three snowballs, scarf, hat, buttons, pipe). Each day, remove one part and ask children to guess what piece is missing. You can make it a mystery by saying, "When I came to class today, I noticed our snowman was missing something. Can you guess?"

Guess What?

Materials/Preparation

* Pre-taped sounds (sounds that are specific to the unit of study)
* Tape recorder

Procedure

As children gather for group time, turn on the tape recorder. The taped sounds you use to grab children's attention should be distinctive and unusual. For example, the elephant's trumpeting call played loudly will get children's attention. Then you can say, "What kind of animal do you think made *that* noise? Listen for the next animal." Repeat this several times. Each time they identify an animal's call, display a picture to reinforce the learning and association. Once you get the group's attention through taped sounds, you can move on to your discussion or introduce the activity.

Variations

Use sounds made with objects connected to a particular theme or discussion topic. For example, play a tape of a running shower or the sound of a hair dryer when discussing health and body care.

Make a Rainbow

Materials/Preparation

* A prism or mirror
* A bright, sunny day

Procedure

Making a rainbow is a novel way to catch children's attention. As children are gathering for group time, use a small hand mirror or a prism to catch the sunshine. Reflect it to a spot on the carpet. You can direct specific children to each spot as you move the light beam. "Suzie can sit on this light ray. Alfonz, you can sit on this light ray." Or you might say, "When you come to circle time, please find a rainbow and sit on it." It is important that you experiment with the prism or mirror before doing this with your group. The sunlight will have to be right in order for this activity to work. It may work for a 10 a.m. gathering but not a 4:00 p.m. story or vice versa.

Variations

As the children are gathering, reflect the rainbow on different parts of the room to see if they can find the light beam.

Props and Things

Materials/Preparation

* Any object(s) used to introduce a story, song, or an interest center. Examples: a real carrot, a large stuffed carrot, or a packet of carrot seeds to introduce *The Carrot Seed* by Ruth Krauss.

Procedure

Ask children to find their places in the circle so they can see. Tell the children that you have brought a special book with you today. Tell them you have a clue about this book. Give them other clues such as, "It's orange and long. You eat it. It's a vegetable." If the children guess it's a carrot, you can say, "You're right, our story is about a carrot!" Then ask two or three children to go into the hallway where you placed a large stuffed carrot or a packet of carrot seeds. Ask them to bring it to the group area. "The name of the book is *The Carrot Seed* by Ruth Krauss."

You have just grabbed the children's attention. They're now ready and you can move right into your story. Repeat this procedure to introduce a new song, science project, or learning center. You don't always have to hide the objects, but it adds to the suspense, grabs their attention, and motivates children to listen.

Variations

Bring children to the object such as a large stump you've had hauled into the play yard, a new piece of equipment, or a new interest center. Perhaps you know someone with a semitrailer truck or pick-up truck with a topper. Ask them to bring their truck to the center or school. Climb inside with your group to read the book *Trucks* by Donald Crews.

Nonsense Statements

Materials/Preparation

* No materials required.

Procedures

You can grab children's attention easily if you are willing to be a little silly. Use your imagination. Create the unexpected for children by saying or doing something that is out of order or doesn't make sense. For example, you can say to children on a wintery day, "You can put on your swimming suit before you go outside," or "You'll need your snow pants," when it's a summer day. On a sunny day you might say, "Look outside, it's a blizzard!" When children notice, they will tell you what is wrong. When you make nonsense statements, use words or ideas that are very different from the expected words. It is easier for children to catch your mistake that way. For example, if swimming is sometimes an option, you have to make sure to use this statement at a time of the year when swimming isn't a choice. This is a good way to encourage children to comment and think critically.

Variations

Another way to get children's attention is to do something silly yourself. For example, pretend to have a hard time getting a lid off a box. Or try to put a record in the tape recorder. In each of these situations, act like nothing is different until the children let you know there is a problem. Then admit your mistake and ask them how to fix it so the activity can go on. Children usually enjoy seeing you being silly. And you will certainly keep their attention.

Specialty Puppets

Materials/Preparation

* A puppet, stuffed animal, or child-sized doll

Procedure

Specialty puppets are distinctive stuffed animals, dolls, or puppets. They visit your classroom for a specific activity, at a specific time of the day, or at certain times of the year. Insure the attention grabbing quality by bringing the puppet out infrequently. The first time the specialty puppet visits be sure to explain to the children the purpose of this visitor. One teacher used a Cabbage Patch doll that came at the beginning of the year to talk about classroom rules. "Clarrisa" returned regularly at first to remind children of the rules. Then she came only when children needed a refresher. She did not appear at any other time.

In one classroom, a baby puppet came the first day of school. It only babbled. As the year progressed, the children taught the baby to talk. They even named the baby. When the baby visited, the children taught it a few more words. They recorded picture words on chart paper so the baby's progress could be watched by the children. The children were thrilled when the baby learned to say their names. The puppet was highly motivating to the children. They excitedly came to group time and requested to get the baby out. It became a ritual to put the baby to bed after the beginning of group time. Then group time would continue.

Variations

Use a book worm puppet (an old hair dryer hose or 2″ tubing covered with green fabric) to introduce a book to the children. Don't use the worm puppet with every book, or it will lose its attention-getting qualities. Choose your specialty puppets carefully and use each sparingly to grab children's attention.

Magical Melodies

Materials/Preparation

* Finger plays set to music
* Records or tapes
* Songbooks

(see appendix A for resources)

Procedure

Music is one of the best attention grabbers you can use. Whether you play a tape, an instrument, or sing a song, children will naturally turn their attention to the music. The songs, tapes, and finger plays listed in appendix A are some of our favorites. Try this little song, "Did You Ever Taste an Apple?" to the tune of "Did You Ever See a Lassie?"

Verse 1

Did you ever taste an apple, an apple, an apple?

Did you ever taste an apple, Oh how did it taste?

Ask children to give you a descriptive word, such as sweet or juicy, and continue singing.

Oh, yes, I tasted an apple, an apple, an apple.

Oh, yes, I tasted an apple. It tasted so sweet.

Verse 2 Smell a rose bud.

Verse 3 See a butterfly.

Verse 4 Feel a caterpillar.

Verse 5 Hear a duck quack.

Look for songs that have actions to keep little hands and fingers busy. These songs will help develop fine motor skills.

Develop your own bag of musical tricks to use when you need the children's attention. Pictures, props or tangibles to go with songs are handy to have in your bag.

Finger Play Book

Materials/Preparation

* Finger Play Book (directions on page 98)

Procedure

Familiar finger plays have an immediate attention grabbing effect. Those with a quick cadence or a loud clap work particularly well. Five little monkeys or five little hot dogs are good examples. A visual aid made to accompany the finger play also focuses and sustains the children's attention. Any finger play that has numbers (first, second, third), shapes, or sizes lends itself well to flannelboard visuals.

As you learn finger plays, create a personal finger play book. This book of 5″ x 8″ cards is a personal collection of your favorites including any new ones you try. Organize them into categories, such as seasons, holidays, or thematic units, to find them easily. The book is easy to glance at as it lays open on your lap. It leaves your hands free to make the appropriate hand movements. Once you have learned the finger play, put the book away. Occasionally review finger plays learned earlier in the year. Children love saying ones that are out of season or from a holiday that has passed.

Variations

Use the following finger play with a garland wand (directions on page 90). Invite five children to line up as snowmen. Invite a sixth child to tap the other children. As each verse is said, use the garland wand to touch the snowman who leaves. This involves all the children in speaking, listening, and following the sequence of the finger play.

Five round snowmen frozen to the core

One fell over, and now there are four.

Four round snowmen, grinning at me

One rolled away, and now there are three.

Three round snowmen, nothing much to do

One disappeared, and now there are two.

Two round snowmen, sitting in the sun

One melted down, and now there is one.

One round snowman, when the day is done

He fell apart, and now there is none.

To Get Started

Capture children's attention by presenting hidden objects with a little mystery and suspense.

Stretchers

I t's raining again! The children in the Little Learners Nursery School can't go out. Mrs. Schwartz has them together in one large group, hoping to keep them interested by reading several books until they go home. She resorted to books because she didn't have anything planned that would replace active outdoor play. She just started reading the book, "Five Little Monkeys Jumping on the Bed," when Sven announced, "That's how I feel, all jumpy inside." Mrs. Schwartz laughed and said, "You'd better save those jumpy feelings until you get home," and continued with the story. She thought to herself, "Will 11:30 ever get here?"

Sometimes, often unintentionally, we push children's attention span to the limit. We think to ourselves, "They seem so interested, I'll just finish this book." Or, "They are sitting so well, I'll just finish the language lesson." To our dismay, five more minutes puts them over the edge. Mrs. Schwartz needs to tune into children's restlessness and anticipate their need to get up and move and stretch.

Using stretchers as a change of pace often averts a management problem. Stretchers are exactly what the word says. Children and adults get up (or remain seated) and stretch out muscles in their bodies. Once they have stretched, they are ready to settle again into the activity. Below are helpful guidelines for using stretchers with children.

Guidelines

1. Tune into the children's behavior. Their restlessness should send a message that you need to take a break from what you are doing.

2. Change the pace *before* children need it. We suggest again that you use the Triple A strategy: Anticipate, Act, and Avert.

3. Empathize with the children's restlessness. Say to them, "I like what we're doing, but I need to get up and get my wiggles out. Let's stretch and then we can finish circle time."

4. Have on hand a variety of props, such as streamers on a stick or beanbags, for times when the wiggles get the best of children. Real objects act as motivators to get children moving.

5. Participate in the stretching activity yourself. Children love it when you act like a monkey with them. Reluctant children are more apt to join in with you.

6. Give children guidelines before you start doing stretchers. This will prevent the likelihood of children getting too silly or carried away with the activity. For example, "When my hand goes up, you need to stop."

7. Resettle children after the stretch and before the group time resumes.

Activities

Stretching, Stretching

Materials/Preparation

★ No materials required.

Procedure

After children have been sitting and concentrating on quiet activities for a time, get them up and do a little stretching. Anticipate and avert potential problems by discussing how the children should space themselves so they are not bumping into one another. For example, "Make sure you are far enough away from your friends so that when you stretch your arms out they are not touching anyone." Make sure they have listened to your guidelines and are ready to move before you begin the song.

Here is a song for stretching arms and bodies you can do when your children get the wiggles:

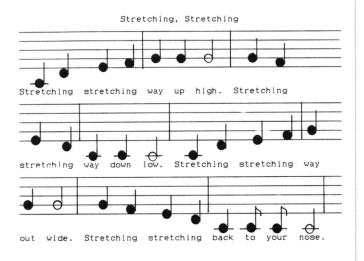

Stretching, Stretching

Stretching stretching way up high. Stretching

stretching way down low. Stretching stretching way

out wide. Stretching stretching back to your nose.

Sing the song at different speeds—sometimes slow, sometimes fast. Change the speed within the same verse. Warn children that you will be doing this as the song progresses so they are prepared to listen and move accordingly. Repeat the song two or three times. Follow it with a settling activity (see chapter 2) to get children gathered again to resume group time.

Variations

Many stretching songs are already recorded for your use. "Head, Shoulders, Knees, and Toes" and "The Noble Duke of York" state specific actions. "Wiggle Wobble" encourages creative movement. See the action song resources in appendix A.

Hoopla

Materials/Preparation

* A hoop for each child (for example, hula hoops, purchased plastic circular hoops, plastic embroidery hoops, rings from a ring toss game)

Procedure

Stretch with hoops of all shapes and sizes. Place the hoop on the floor. The children do stretching actions around or in it. Hop, walk, run, gallop, and tiptoe in and around the hoop. Put a foot, two hands, a foot and a hand, or nose and a finger in the hoop.

Play music as children dance among the hoops. When the music stops, children find a hoop to stand in until it starts again.

Guide children to hold the hoop around one leg, their head, two arms, their waist, or a finger. Encourage them to twirl it on their arm (older children should be able to do this) or shake it to the music (attach streamers and/or jingle bells for added attention).

There are albums, tapes, CDs, and books that have hoop activities. What happy hoopla times children can have!

Variations

Have older children play cooperatively with a hoop by rolling it back and forth among each other.

When you have only one large hoop and a large group of children, stand in a circle and roll the hoop to a designated child. Continue until all children have had a chance to catch and roll the hoop.

Guide children to sit in a circle and place the hoop in the middle. One child stands in the hoop and does an action. The children in the circle imitate the action.

Give them problem-solving situations, such as "How can we get five hands in this one hoop?" After the problem is solved ask them, "Can this be done in a different way? And yet another way?"

Keep on rolling with creative ideas.

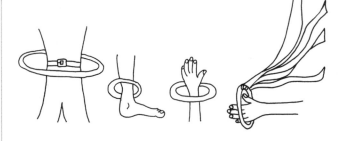

Up and Down

Materials/Preparation

* No materials required.

Procedure

Arms and legs get the action in this stretching activity. When you see children's interest waning, guide them to sit flat on the floor, legs extended. Recite the chant below while stretching the legs. Now stand with arms at side. Repeat chant while stretching arms. Finally, ask children to sit and repeat leg stretches.

Up, down. (raise legs/arms up and down)

Up, down. (repeat action)

Up, down. (repeat action)

And all around. (legs/arms make circular motion)

In, out. (legs/arms close to body and push out in front)

In, out. (repeat action)

In, out. (repeat action)

And swing about. (swing legs/arms back and forth in front of body)

Chant at different speeds and repeat as many times as necessary for your group to get all their wiggles out. Ending with the children in a sitting position makes it easier to get them settled for the rest of group time.

Variations

This variation gets the arms exercising.

Stretch to the left. (stretch both arms to your left)

Stretch to the right. (stretch both arms to your right)

Now in front. (stretch both arms out in front of body)

Then out of sight. (hide arms behind back)

If your children don't know the difference between left and right, place a small sticker on their right hand or model correct directions by turning around with your back to the children as you recite the words and do the actions.

Streamers on a Stick

Materials/Preparation

* A streamer for each child and yourself (directions on pages 85–6)

* Streamer activities resources (see appendix A)

Procedure

Streamers help children's bodies move. Even inhibited children become so interested in making and watching the streamer move that they don't realize their bodies are in action or they are dancing. Model fun and action, especially for the more hesitant children.

Streamers cut in approximately 12″ lengths can act as a motivational visual aid. Choose colors that tie into your theme or strengthen a concept you are teaching such as colors. Tell the children to wave or shake their streamer above their head, down by their toes, behind them, and between their legs. Direct children to shake them fast or slow.

Play music and have children move (with their streamers) to the rhythm. Tell the children to stop when the music stops. Turn the music on again and proceed with the actions.

Sing this song to the tune "Put Your Finger in the Air."

Shake your streamer in the air, in the air.

Shake your streamer in the air, in the air.

Shake your streamer in the air, shake your streamer in the air, shake your streamer in the air, in the air.

Wave your streamer by the ground, by the ground.

Wave your streamer by the ground, by the ground.

Wave your streamer by the ground, wave your streamer by the ground, wave your streamer by the ground, by the ground.

Variations

Two streamers, one for each hand, promote new and interesting actions. Wave them back and forth crossing hands over each other. Shake one in front and one in back. Let the children's creative imagination float and flow with this versatile item.

Follow Me

Materials/Preparation

* No materials required.

Procedure

You sense that it will soon be time for the children to get up and stretch. One clue is that your own body is feeling restless. Encourage children to imitate you doing different actions. Sing the following fun song as you move and stretch. "Follow Me" is to the same tune as "Clean-Up Time" found in part 2, chapter 1.

FOLLOW ME

Follow me. Follow me. Everyone follow me. Follow me.
Follow me. Do the action that you see.

Continue singing the song as long as you think the children need to stretch. Change the action each time. Some actions include hopping, jumping jacks, clapping, or swaying.

Settle children with a final quieting action. Sit with hands in lap or tap your index fingers as you whisper the song and slow the pace.

Variations

Say this little chant as directions to get the children moving with you: "Follow, follow, follow me. Do the action that you see."

Quickly say the chant and do the actions for a short period of time. Repeat the chant and move to another action.

Super Stretchies

Materials/Preparation

★ A stretchy for each child and yourself (directions are on page 98)

Procedure

Stretchies are great fun and promote creative movement. Give each child a stretchy and guide them to do specific tasks with it. Let them think up their own actions. Model for the children as you give them directions. Some ideas are listed below.

Stretch your stretchy:

★ with two hands

★ with one hand and one foot

★ with one hand and two feet

★ so it makes the numeral 1

★ so it makes the numeral 8

★ so it makes a triangular shape

★ so it makes the letter V

★ with another child and their stretchy to make the numeral 10

Guide two children to sit down on the floor facing each other with their feet together and both holding on to the same stretchy. One child lies down as the other child bends forward. Have them go back and forth helping each other do sit-ups. This is a good cooperative activity.

Note: Supervise children using stretchies so they don't put them around their neck.

Variations

Make a merry-go-round with your group of children and their stretchies. Take a ring (a rubber ring from a ring toss works well or a macramé hoop) and have each child wrap their stretchy through and around it. Now have each child hang onto both ends of their stretchy with one hand. All the children face in the same direction. As the music begins, they gallop around in a circle as if they were the horses on a merry-go-round. Play music similar to a merry-go-round sound or sing this song to the tune of "Row, Row, Row Your Boat."

Gallop, gallop, gallop around.

Gallop around the ring.

Gallop, gallop, gallop around. Gallop around I sing.

Use other actions such as trot or walk.

Clap, Clap, Tap, Tap

Materials/Preparation

★ No materials required.

Procedure

Anticipate when children need a break and avert problems by including a stretcher in your group time planning. This finger play includes a variety of actions. Children move their hands, feet, and arms.

Clap, clap, (clap hands)

Tap, tap, (tap floor with toe)

Stretch up high, reach the sky. (stretch arms up)

Clap, clap, (clap hands)

Tap, tap, (tap floor with toe)

Bend down low, touch your toe. (bend at waist and touch toes)

Do this action rhyme at different speeds. Start out slowly and challenge the children by asking them to do it a little faster. Increase speed until you think they have reached their peak.

Using the new words below, recite the words one more time, slowly, to get the children seated and relaxed.

Clap, clap,

Tap, tap,

Sit on the rug, give yourself a hug.

(Or Sit down flat, on the mat; or Sit on the floor, let's do no more.)

Variations

Although clapping and tapping are reasonable actions, change them when children seem to be ready for something different. Some other actions that fit into the chant include hop, pat, jump, stomp, and so on.

Wand Stop and Go

Materials/Preparation

* A wand (directions for making felt star, heart, and fall leaf wands; looped fabric stop and go wands; and Styrofoam ball spider wands are found on pages 87 to 89)

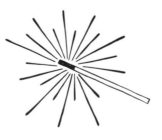

Procedure

Use your wand to magically and visually guide children through their stretching activities. Tell them to watch the wand so they know when to start and stop. Wave it over the children to cue them for stretching activities. Combine any of the other stretching ideas with the wand such as singing and moving, or moving like an animal that is displayed on the felt board. Then wave the wand to indicate that they should stop stretching. A stop and go wand facilitates this activity.

Different wands encourage varying movements. Use a star wand to sing "Twinkle, Twinkle, Little Star." Children float around on their tiptoes, wave their arms, and wiggle their fingers as if they were a star high in the sky.

A heart wand promotes exercises like jumping jacks and running in place that give you a healthy heart.

With a colorful leaf wand ask the children to pretend they are leaves falling from an autumn tree. They can float and blow around as if they were being carried away by the wind, and finally swirl quietly to the floor as if they were landing on the ground. Use the wand to show children these actions.

The spider wand accompanying the song "The Eency Weency Spider" encourages creeping around like a tiny spider. Repeat the song in a louder voice and sing and move about like a middle-sized spider, and very loudly and slowly like a great big spider.

Variations

Use the wand for tapping children during a stretching activity. Position children in a circle and tap one child with the wand. That child goes into the middle of the circle, does a movement, and all of the other children imitate him. Have them continue this exercise until you tap another child for their turn to be in the middle. Continue the tapping process until you feel the children have gotten enough movement, then tap yourself and sit down. All the children will imitate your movement to end the stretching activity.

Pick a Moving Card

Materials/Preparation

* Laminated 5" x 7" or 8" x 10" purchased or hand-drawn pictorial cards with different body

movements such as tap head, bend knees, touch toes, wiggle hips, shake arms, kick legs, or roll head around.

★ A bag (a paper bag, school bag, or shopping bag) or other storage container; design the bag or container to coordinate with a theme.

Procedure

It's nice to give children the opportunity to make choices for stretching activities, but sometimes they have difficulty thinking of a movement. In cases such as these, use cards with the names and pictures of body actions.

As the children are sitting in group or standing in anticipation, invite one child to come up and pull a card out of the decorative bag or container.

If the child can read or understands the picture, have them name the action. The child stands at the front of the group and leads everyone in the exercise. Use a timer for each body action. Have another child choose a card and begin again.

Variations

Use an apron with a big pocket to store your cards. Put a button, snap, or strip of hooked fasteners at the top of the pocket. When you do exercises with the children, your cards won't fall out. Directions for making a pocket apron (variation two) are on page 100.

Be Bop with Beanbags

Materials/Preparation

★ A beanbag for each child and yourself (directions on page 95)

★ Beanbag activity resources (see appendix A)

Procedure

Beanbags promote action. Give each child a beanbag to do some stretching and get their wiggles out. Many beanbag resources have songs for individual beanbag games.

There are many activities to do with beanbags. Have the children balance their beanbag on different parts of their body such as their head, elbow, knee, back, or nose. Count to five or have them walk around as they do their balancing act.

Call out some directions for the children to follow as they are holding their beanbag. Start out with one direction at a time. As they master one, move on to two and so on. Following are some examples of directions.

★ Place your beanbag on your head.

★ Tap your knee with your beanbag.

★ Touch your head and then your toe with your beanbag.

★ Toss your beanbag in the air and then place it behind you.

★ Put your beanbag on your shoulder, knock it off, and jump over it.

These directions will test their comprehension and receptive language skills.

After all this beanbag exercise, children will be ready to return to group time activities. Have children place beanbags in a storage bucket.

Variations

Encourage cooperative play between partners. Have them toss the beanbag to each other, or take turns throwing the beanbag in a bucket. One child can throw the beanbag and the other can retrieve it.

See if two children can hold the beanbag between them with just their knees, or between one child's elbow and the other child's tummy.

What's in the Egg?

Materials/Preparation

★ Plastic eggs that open up

★ Small strips of paper with actions drawn or written on them

★ Basket or other container

Procedure

Here is another creative way to get children up and moving when the need strikes. In each egg, place a strip of paper with actions written or drawn on them. Fill a basket with plastic eggs. Have a child come up and choose an egg out of the basket. (You can ask them to select a certain color to check color concept recognition.) Ask the child to open the egg and pull out the strip of paper. Read the action or have the child look at the picture. Have the child tell the class what action they are to do. Some examples are listed below.

* **Do five jumping jacks.**
* **Do seven sit-ups.**
* **Do four knee bends.**
* **Do ten toe touches.**

Ask two children to come up and each pick an egg out of the basket. This gives children an opportunity to hear and follow two directions.

Variations

Instead of eggs, put your actions strips in a hat, bag, or tin. Whatever the container, children enjoy the surprise hidden inside.

Movin' with the Cube

Materials/Preparation

* Looped fabric cube (directions on page 101)
* Pieces to put on the cube, such as numerals, pictures of body parts, colors, or picture cards with actions on them

Procedure

Bring out your cube to encourage stretching when the wiggles have gotten the best of children. There are many ways the cube can facilitate action.

Create dice by placing numerals on the cubes. Have a child toss the cube. Whatever numeral turns up is the number of times the group will do a particular action. The child who tossed the cube chooses an action, such as hop five times. The advantage of the cube is that you can select the numbers you want, unlike a regular dice with non-removable dots. Encourage more exercise by placing numbers seven through twelve on the cube. If you have two cubes, roll both and add the two numbers together to determine the number of actions.

Another way to use two cubes is by putting numerals on one and action pictures on the other. Have two children roll one cube each. Then complete the action to match the number that was rolled. For example, if one cube showed "clap your hands" and the other showed the numeral six, the children would clap their hands six times.

Pictures of body parts on the cube offer another choice. Invite a child to roll the cube. She chooses what everyone will do with the body part that appears, such as wiggle your fingers or bend your knees.

Colors on the cube add another variation. Again have a child roll the cube. If the color blue comes up, tell children wearing blue to stand up and do ten jumping jacks. Put common colors of clothing on the cube so many children get to exercise.

Keep on moving creatively with the cube!

Variations

Combine some other stretcher ideas with the cube. Roll the cube to determine the number of times children will throw and catch their beanbag or leap in the hoop.

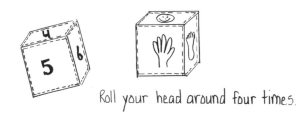

Roll your head around four times.

Move Around the Mats

Materials/Preparation

* Movement mats (directions on page 102)
* Record player/tape recorder
* Record/tape

Procedure

"Move Around the Mats" is similar to the game "Musical Chairs." In this version, however, don't take away mats like you do with musical chairs. Keep everyone playing. This eliminates competition and the labeling of some children as winners and some as losers. Free movement and letting the children's imaginations flow is the key to this activity.

Lay the mats on the floor randomly in the group area (these replace the chairs). Ask the children to find a mat to stand on. Tell the children when the music starts to get off and move freely around the mats (dancing, hopping, skipping, or galloping). When the music stops they find a new mat to stand on. While the children are relaxing briefly, ask some children what numeral they are standing on. Start the music again and repeat as long as you think the children need to move.

After this activity, ask children to pick up the mat they were standing on and put it away. This gives them a small responsibility and enables you to get ready for the next activity while they are working on that task. Do a brief settling activity from chapter 2 as children return to their individual spaces.

Variations

Foam rubber place mats are durable and versatile. Change the numerals to letters, colors, shapes, or symbols of a particular theme to make qualitative plus quantitative use of them.

Hop Little Bunnies

Materials/Preparation

* No materials required.

Procedure

If you want a lot of action, this is the song for you. It involves various animals and how they move. Introduce new vocabulary such as creeping kitties, slithering snakes, and galloping horses.

Children will need plenty of room for this stretching activity, but also remember to give them boundaries to move in, such as staying on the carpeted area.

Sing the following songs to the tune "Mary Had A Little Lamb."

Verse 1

Hop little bunny, hop, hop, hop,

Hop, hop, hop,

Hop, hop, hop.

Hop little bunny, hop, hop, hop. Hop around the room.

Verse 2 Slither little snake, slither, slither, slither…

Verse 3 Gallop little horsey, gallop, gallop, gallop…

Verse 4 Run little doggy, run, run, run…

Verse 5 Waddle little ducky, waddle, waddle, waddle…

Change the last sentence of the last verse to "Waddle back to the group."

Be aware of your group as this stretcher is very active. If you sense children getting out of control, end the activity. Group size is also an important consideration. This activity is best done with a small number of children (five to seven).

Variations

Using the tune "Mary Had A Little Lamb" again, have children do basic movements. Ask them to tiptoe, dance, march, stamp, sway, jump, or skate.

Tiptoe my friends, tiptoe, tiptoe, tiptoe,

Tiptoe, tiptoe, tiptoe,

Tiptoe, tiptoe, tiptoe.

Tiptoe my friends, tiptoe, tiptoe, tiptoe. Tiptoe around the room.

Old Favorites

Materials/Preparation

* Cassette tape and tape recorder
* Exercise tapes (see appendix A)

Procedure

There's nothing like moving to old favorite songs—those that children ask to have played over and over. Prerecord some of their favorite stretching activities on cassette tapes. Sing, play instruments, or chant several activities on the same tape. Have it available when children become restless. Children can also use the tape, on their own, during free play time.

Commercially made exercise tapes are also excellent choices. Some of these include directions and pictures of different actions to go with the songs—use those or make up your own.

Add a few settling songs to the tape for regrouping children. "I Stretch My Hands" from chapter 2 is an excellent choice.

Variations

Use popular songs that children are familiar with to do selected movements. As the tempo of the song changes, so can the movements. It is a good idea to have consistent movements for different sections of the song. One word of caution—preview the words in popular songs. Make sure your choices are appropriate to use with children.

Making Tracks

Materials/Preparation

★ No materials required.

Procedure

Ask children to pretend that they are moving on a variety of surfaces as you describe the situations. Here are some statements to encourage creative movement:

★ "Someone just spilled maple syrup on the kitchen floor. Try walking on it—steady!"

★ "It has just started to snow outside and you are getting ready to walk home. Start out very slowly because it might be slippery."

★ "Rain has filled your garden with water and it's time to pick your vegetables. Show how you would move carefully through the mud. Slosh!"

★ "Walk around the circle and imagine that you are on hot sand at the beach."

Include a variety of movements. It is also important to bring closure to the stretcher activity and direct the children to make tracks back to the gathering space.

Variations

Ask the children to move as if on bare feet, wearing boots, or with skates.

To Get Started:

Take a break once in awhile. Give those muscles a good stretch.

Extenders

Mr. Gonzales and his group of children at the Moving Right Along Head Start have had a busy morning. They had just finished a story that took less time than he had planned. Then, the cook informed them that lunch would be five minutes late. Mr. Gonzales looked at his staff and said, "Looks like we have to get out our tap shoes." Because he hadn't anticipated the extra time, he didn't know what to do. He asked the children if they wanted to sing "If You're Happy" again. In a chorus, they replied, "No!" Next he asked, "Well, what would you like to do while we wait?" Jason and La Mont started wrestling on the floor. Several children left the group and started taking toys off the shelf. He took the hands of a couple of children and led them over to the lunch table with the hopes the others would follow. "Now where are those tap shoes?" he thought to himself.

We have all had a similar experience of having extra time on our hands with the whole group. How do you hold their attention? How do you keep them focused long enough so you can make a smooth transition to the next activity?

Anticipate the possibility of extra time. For these unexpected gaps in the schedule where you have the whole group, we suggest you plan extenders. Extenders are activities that extend or expand children's knowledge about a current theme or topic. Plan activities with your current theme in mind (dinosaurs, families, etc.). Or use extenders to reinforce concepts taught earlier in the year, such as numbers or colors. Use some of the guidelines below to help you plan your extenders.

Guidelines

1. Recognize that this is one of those times that you have to provide a little teacher direction so as to maintain order as children wait.

2. Include in your lesson plan ideas for extending activities. This is good insurance should your lesson run a few minutes short. For example, props like flannelboards, little games, and songs with visuals are fun to use while children wait.

3. Prepare props and games that reinforce basic color, number, pre-reading, and language concepts. Keep them close at hand.

4. Choose extender activities that actively involve all the children.

5. Avoid using books to "fill in the time." This use of books takes the value and joy away from reading.

Activities

Animal Hunt

Materials/Preparation

* A small stuffed animal hidden before the group time.

Procedure

Take a few minutes before a group time to hide a stuffed animal in your classroom. Take care so no children see your preparation. As group time is winding down and you have a few minutes before the next activity begins, ask children to move around the room and look for the hidden stuffed animal.

Give them clues and tell them when they are getting close to the hidden animal. Say, "The special mouse is hiding in a very musical place. This place is also a spot where the teacher sits during music time" (piano bench). Instruct the children to signal with a clap, clap when they see the hidden animal and return to group time. When most of the group has found the animal, use it to introduce the next activity.

Variations

Choose one child to close his eyes or leave the room as the teacher or another child hides an animal. The child opens his eyes or returns and attempts to find the animal. The remaining children let the finder know if he is close to the hidden animal by humming.

What's Beneath the Bowl?

Materials/Preparation

* Three to five bowls or cups of different colors and sizes.

* One small object to put under the bowls, such as a pom-pom pal (directions on page 102)

Procedure

It's true—sometimes we wish we could do magic like the famed magicians. As long as most of us don't have these skills, we'll have to settle for the next best thing. Try this activity that has been adapted from a magician's trick.

Place three to five bowls upside down in front of you, where all children can see. Have the children shut their eyes. Tuck a small object under one of the bowls. Tell children they may open their eyes now. Ask a child to guess which bowl the object is under. Pick up the bowl to see if their guess was right. If it wasn't, ask another child. Continue until the object is found. Repeat the game, and just like magic, before you know, it will be time to move on to the next activity.

Use bowls that are different colors or sizes, so children can make a reference to their guess. "Is the pom-pom pal under the green bowl?" Mark your bowls with stickers or permanent markers if they are the same size and color. Margarine tubs are a good, recycled choice for this activity.

Choose an object to hide that has been used during group time. This is one more way to reinforce the topic discussed. It also is a way to make multiple use of your props.

Because this is a quick moving activity, children will be actively involved. Strive to give children many guesses.

Variations

Wear an apron with several pockets as an alternative to the bowls. Have different colored buttons on the pockets so children can label their guess. "Is it in the blue button pocket?" Directions for making a pocket apron (variation 1) are on page 99.

When you don't have any cups or aprons available, hold the object in one hand. Have children point to the hand they think the object is in. Small rocks, rhinestones, or pom-pom pals fit nicely in your hand.

Pick and Choose a Song

Materials/Preparation

* A list of songs children know; add to the list as they learn new ones.

* A song-choosing visual aid, such as a window shade chart, song flowers, or deck of songs (directions on pages 103 to 104)

Procedure

Children enjoy singing favorite songs over and over again. Make a list of all of the songs (or favorite songs) that your children know. When you have a few minutes at the end of group, have a child choose a song and everyone sing it. Action songs are great.

Make your list on a window shade. Roll it up on the rod and put it away when necessary. Remember to use permanent markers on the shade so it does not smear.

Make your list on a long strip of paper. Laminate it if you intend to leave it up for a period of time. Attach more sheets as you and the children learn new songs.

Add pictures on the song list so that nonreaders can make their own choices. Put a lamb by "Mary Had A Little Lamb," a spider by "The Eency Weency Spider," or a smiling face by "If You're Happy and You Know It". Children can help with illustrations.

Variations

If you don't have a large enough space to hang a window shade or paper chart, consider some of the alternatives listed.

* Make some poster board song flowers with the names of songs written on them. Place them in a vase for children to pick.

* Write the children's favorite songs on small strips of paper. Fold them and insert each one in a balloon. Blow up the balloons and knot the ends. Ask a child to pop a balloon and find the song strip inside. Remember to throw away all balloon pieces.

* Make a deck of cards out of poster board and write the name of each song on a card and add pictures. Tuck your deck of cards into an apron pocket for children to draw from. Directions for making pocket aprons are on page 99.

* A music booklet is another variation. Children can flip through the pages until they find a song they like. Directions for making a music booklet and easel are on page 93.

Children will enjoy this activity whether they choose a particular song or are surprised, such as with popping a balloon.

Calendar Picture Fun

Materials/Preparation

* Mount calendar pictures on poster board. Cover with clear contact paper.

Procedure

Use spare minutes at the end of a group activity to promote language skills by getting children involved in a discussion about the mounted photos and pictures you show them. Take advantage of the many good deals found on outdated calendars at your local bookstores and stationery shops.

Share pictures with the children to initiate a story or a lively discussion about the items or people in them. For example, an autumn scene with children frolicking in brightly colored leaves blowing in the wind encourages discussion about the autumn weather and fun. Action photos or pictures depicting people with expressive faces often start interesting story lines. Show a picture of a child opening a present and ask the children to think about the object in the wrapped package.

Guide their responses with open-ended sentences that they can complete. "I think the present would be…" "Great, it's a…" Their responses and comments will be insightful. Make sure the items in the pictures are large and easily seen by the children.

Variations

Mount recycled greeting cards on poster board to elicit responses from the children.

Wand Shape Walk

Materials/Preparation

* Three to four wands (felt star wand or triangle, circle, or square looped fabric wand); directions on pages 87 to 89

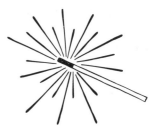

Procedure

Wands offer an excellent opportunity to motivate children and make good use of extra time while extending learning and reinforcing skills.

Prepare wands with a variety of shapes (star, triangle, circle, square). Give wands to several children and instruct the group to watch as those children look for objects whose shape corresponds with the shape of the wand they carry. Encourage them to find a variety of items. Include all of the children as you ask them to help with ideas.

The circle wand helps the children hunt for circular items such as a plate set on the table for lunch, a clock on the wall, a trampoline on the floor, a block on the shelf, and a paperweight on the director's desk. With the square wand, find square items, such as a book, game board, table, and papers. Use a star wand and look around in an outdoor setting. Spot flowers shaped like stars, a pattern on a child's shirt, or chalk stars on the pavement.

Children gently tap the objects as they find them. Acknowledge their attempts and discoveries. What a fun way to explore and find success!

Variations

Encourage cooperative learning. Direct the children to work in pairs to find items to match their wand. As one pair finds an item, the wand is held over it until other groups find that shape.

Spinner Board Stories

Materials/Preparation

* Spinner story board and shapes (directions on page 104)

Procedure

Provide active participation for children when you have some time left with the group and your planned activities are completed. The spinner board offers a flexible and tangible item to use when expanding your instructional times.

Explain that the group will use the spinner board to help tell a story. Spin the arrow to a particular shape or piece. Start a story or ask a child to begin. For example, when the spinner points to a cow, start the action and say, "The black and white cow was running to the river." Another person takes a turn and spins the arrow. The next piece turns out to be the sun. A child adds, "The sun dried up the river and the cow was very thirsty."

Continue to involve children and create a story. Accept their ideas and be ready for some very unusual story lines. Create brief stories or continue until each child gets a turn, as time permits.

Variations

Attach characters from favorite stories such as "The Three Bears" or "Little Red Riding Hood" to initiate new versions for the familiar stories.

Cheerful Chants

Materials/Preparation

* Three or four objects or pictures of your choice.

Procedure

The children haven't finished in the bathroom, and the cots aren't set out, but you're done with your planned activities. Don't panic. Use theme-related materials to extend the activity time, as well as expand the children's minds.

When working on a particular theme, you probably have acquired pictures, real objects, or visual aids that relate to the unit. Take three or four of them and line them up in front of you and the children. Have the children name them. Then, proceeding from left to right, chant the names of the items in a rhythmic pattern. Repeat the chant four or five times. Switch the objects or visual aids around and chant the new line up from left to right. When talking about fruits, use real, artificial, or photographs when reciting this chant:

apple   orange   pineapple   peach

orange   peach   apple   pineapple

In this simple activity, children are exposed to pre-reading, language, music, and pre-math skills. They are also learning the names of fruits in a fun and interesting way. Have them clap with the rhythm to get a better feel of it.

Variations

If you have two pictures or objects of the same item (two balloons, two oranges, two suns, etc.) you can do a matching game. Hand out one of each item to the children. Someone will get a balloon, another will get an orange, and so on. Place a piece of yarn on the floor and line your objects on it. Lay another piece of yarn on the floor parallel to your line and have the children bring their objects up one at a time and place them on the line so that their line matches yours. Repeat by changing the placement of your objects and giving new children a turn.

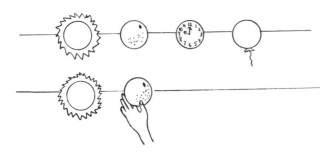

Animal Take Away

Materials/Preparation

* Food props; either plastic, papier-mâché, or poster board pieces

Procedure

This quick game is adapted from a favorite childhood game, "Doggie, Doggie, Where's Your Bone?" Use it to extend your group time; in this activity all children are actively involved. Choose one child to be the first animal, a parrot. Have the parrot sit on a chair, holding and munching a cracker in her home. This child then closes his eyes and pretends to sleep. Another child, whom the teacher has pointed to, takes the cracker, and hides it behind her back. All children put hands behind their backs so the parrot does not know who has the food. The group of children chant, "Parrot, Parrot, do you know, where, oh, where did your cracker go?" At that point, the child portraying the parrot opens his eyes and begins to guess which child has taken the food. Giggles, glances, and pointing fingers are certain to give a few clues. When the one taking the food has been found, that child becomes another animal and the game goes on. Try to give turns to as many children as time permits.

Other animal and food combinations include a horse and carrot, monkey and banana, elephant and peanut, and seal and fish. Use a chant, "Animal, Animal, (fill in the animal name) do you know? Where, oh, where did your food (fill in food) go." Be sure to give yourself a turn to be the sleeping animal. Children thoroughly enjoy working together and fooling the teacher.

Variations

Use the children's names instead of animals. Any object could be used to fit the theme. "Jenni, Jenni, where's your ball? Guess, oh, guess if you know at all." Try also, a comb for a healthy body theme, circles for a shape theme, or flowers for a spring theme.

Name That Crooner

Materials/Preparation

* Tape recorder
* Tape of children singing

Procedure

Help children create their own extender activity. When they have learned several songs rather well, record individual children singing. When you have a few minutes left at the end of group time, turn the tape recorder on and listen. Have children guess who is singing and then join in to finish the song. If they haven't guessed by the time the song ends, give them some hints, like their hair color, or what they are wearing that day. Continue with the tape until it is time to move to the next activity.

This activity encourages children to use their listening skills and learn the uniqueness of individuals. Children also like to hear themselves on tape; it builds their self-esteem.

Variations

Have children talk into the recorder giving clues to who they are or telling a joke. The other children try to guess who is talking.

Flannelboard Action

Materials/Preparation

* Flannelboard
* Large simple felt shapes

Procedure

Play a quick flannelboard game with children in this extender activity. Direct children to identify three to five large familiar shapes or objects as you place them on the board. Choose items that relate to a particular story, season, or curriculum theme. During the spring months, use shapes such as a bird, sun, flower, rabbit, and

duck. Instruct the children to cover their eyes as you remove one or more of the shapes. Remove the pieces, hiding them behind your back or behind the flannelboard. Signal the children to open their eyes and identify the missing piece or pieces. Replace pieces and repeat or add new or different ones.

Variations

Try this extender with a large face on the flannelboard. Remove parts of the face and have the children guess what is missing.

Select another item relating to curriculum theme, such as a jack-o-lantern or snowman. Remove portions from them and direct the children to reassemble the incomplete characters.

1-2-3 Uno, Dos, Tres

Materials/Preparation

* Knowledge of foreign language

Procedure

Learning to communicate in a second language is a source of fun and pride for young children. Make good use of precious moments at the end of a group activity to introduce or review terms in another language.

Begin the study of a new language with common terms including the following: hello, good-bye, mother, father, and numbers. When presenting Spanish terms, start with the following words: hello: hola (oh-la); good-bye: adios (ah-dee-os); My name is: Me llamo es (Mee yamo es); one, two, three, four, five: uno (oo-noh), dos (dohs), tres (trehs), quatro (kwah-troh), cinco (seen-ko); table: mesa (may-sa); girl: nina (nee-nya); boy: nino (nee-nyo). See appendix C for other words and their translations.

Young children are able and enthusiastic learners when it comes to a new language. If you have some

children who already know another language, encourage them to teach the others. These children help their classmates learn their native language while they acquire more skill in the English language. What a boost to everyone's self-esteem and appreciation of cultural diversity.

Variations

Direct children to watch you as you share general body language. Children know some gestures or movements that tell people to look (pointing finger), stop (hand up—palm forward), or go (finger pointed away from the body). After sharing the body language for several days, introduce American Sign Language. You and the children can learn and practice this language in a relaxed manner, day by day. Try to learn some simple songs in American Sign Language, also. See appendix A for resource books.

Group Color Bingo

Materials/Preparation

* Group color bingo game (directions on page 104)

Procedure

Often, as we complete a group time, we find ourselves with several minutes before we can move on to the next activity. This extender is flexible, allowing you options for its use.

Direct children to work together as a group, cooperatively. Hang up the large color bingo game board so all of the children can see it easily. Depending

Red	Orange	Brown
Green	Yellow	Black
Purple	White	Blue

on the time you have and the ages of the children, decide the number of squares you will want to cover. Cover a pattern, such as three colors in a row horizontally, vertically, or diagonally. If you have more time, cover all of the squares. Be sure everyone understands the plan for the day.

One child starts by selecting a color card from a container. Children will look and see if that color is needed to complete the selected pattern. The child brings the piece to the board and attaches it to the hook fastener on the appropriate color square. Repeat this step until you have covered the squares desired. Applaud yourselves—you had success!

Variations

Try stickers or shapes related to a curriculum theme on the squares and make matching cards.

Packing Up

Materials/Preparation

* Small suitcase

Procedure

Take children on an impromptu and imaginary trip when you have some time left after a group activity. This idea expands the learning process.

Seat children in a circle and show them an empty suitcase. Explain that they are all going on a special journey and need to pack the suitcase. Set the scene, using ideas offered by the group. Decide cooperatively where you are going, whom you will visit, and any other interesting particulars. For example, everyone decides to visit grandma's house at the beach. What fun! The first person starts by putting one imaginary item in the suitcase. She says her name out loud, along with the name of the item. "I'm Christina and I'm putting a bottle of sun tanning lotion in the suitcase." Pass the suitcase around and ask each child to add an item. Encourage appropriate responses for the trip, but be sensitive to individual choices.

Each person will add an item and state their name. "I'm Andy and I'm putting a comb in the suitcase." As a group, repeat the list of people and items as you go along. This prevents any one child from being put on the spot to remember all of the names and items. It also allows the children to function as a group. Great memory work!

Other trip destinations could include another planet, the desert, a friend's house, or summer camp.

Variations

Bring a suitcase packed with items and let the children look for a few minutes while you mention the items. Then close the suitcase and direct the children to remember what they saw.

Use a basket and ask the children to prepare a picnic. Have them use their critical thinking skills to determine what items would be inside.

Sing a Standing Song

Materials/Preparation

* No materials required.

Procedure

Active involvement is abundant in this singing game. This song is a great choice no matter where you are or where you are going. It is to the magical tune you have heard in Chapters 1, 2, and 4.

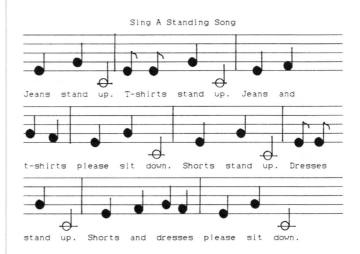

Sing A Standing Song

Jeans stand up. T-shirts stand up. Jeans and t-shirts please sit down. Shorts stand up. Dresses stand up. Shorts and dresses please sit down.

Sing the song slowly so children have time to respond to the directions. Some children will be standing up and sitting down frequently depending on the clothes they are wearing. Sing other characteristics, such as ages, colors on clothing, or colors of hair. Yes, this simple song has many possibilities.

Variations

If you have a little more time and props close by, adapt the song to the new situation. Give each child a shape card and replace clothing with circles, rectangles, triangles, and squares.

To Get Started:

Plan extenders in case you have extra time on your hands.

Magic Carpet Activities

Maggie had eight children in her family child care; their ages ranged from nine months to five years. Six of the children had been working on a special project for Mother's Day. Two still needed help with their project. Two others started chasing each other around the kitchen. Two were hiding behind the couch and three-year-old Mai was crying. While Maggie was checking on the baby, the glitter dish fell off the table. Maggie wailed, "I can't be everywhere at once!!"

How can we make this potential waste time productive and the transition an orderly one? You can make many self-correcting and easy to use activities for children. We call these magic carpet activities. Such activities include file folder games or buddy buckets that encourage independent choice making, develop skills, and promote cooperative play. When children finish a project and are waiting for others, they select from a special shelf (used only for this situation) of these age-appropriate activities. Because this type of activity does not require direct supervision, Maggie can tend to the children who need her immediate attention while children use wait time constructively.

The activities in this chapter include ideas and directions to make your own collection of magic carpet activities. We hope that your children will enjoy them as much as ours. Following are some guidelines for the magic carpet activities.

Guidelines

1. Develop activities designed for individual or partner play. Some examples include tiny tin activities, file folder matching games, or a photo book. Choose activities that have a calming effect.

2. Include some activities that are self-correcting; ones where you do not need to be there to help the children. This type of activity promotes a sense of positive self-worth in the child, "I did it myself!"

3. Keep the activities in a special place where children can easily get and return them.

4. Pair children together for a specific purpose. Ask a child who has good language skills to play a game with a child with delayed language development.

5. Provide special seating places on which one or two children can sit when playing the game of their choice. Call this the buddy rug or the magic carpet.

Activities

Magic Carpet Places

Materials/Preparation

* Magic carpets. Make magic carpets from a variety of materials. Use hand towels, carpet squares, place mats or sit-upons. Use 24" x 24" or 36" x 36" squares of brightly colored fabric, a vinyl tablecloth, or a shower curtain. Ask children to decorate the tablecloth or shower curtain with permanent magic markers.

Procedure

Create a variety of magic carpet activities for children to choose from and use them when children have to wait for others to finish a previous task or routine. Children should be able to use most of them independently or with a partner. Store the activities on a special shelf or in a crate. Usually, magic carpet activities are not available at other times of the day.

Variations

Use child-sized beanbags, squares of material, carpet squares, or the sit-upons described in "Places and

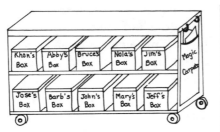

Spaces" in chapter 2 to create your magic carpets. A large cardboard barrel, with an opening cut in the side at the bottom, makes a special place for doing quiet activities. Children occasionally need time and space by themselves during a busy day.

Folder Fun

Materials/Preparation

* ⋆ Several file folder games (directions on pages 104–6)
* ⋆ File folder resource books (see appendix A)

Procedure

Magic carpet activities begin when some children finish the group activity. They choose an educational folder game until the rest of the group has finished. Folder activities include all necessary parts so children can manipulate them without your assistance. They are flat for efficient storage and easy for children to get out and return. The first few times folder games are used, show children where the pieces are stored and where to put them back.

Provide folder activities that are at the children's developmental level. Any of the folder activities are appropriate for older preschoolers; they can reinforce concepts you are currently teaching. If you know a child understands a concept, encourage him to pair up with a friend who still needs some practice in that area. Instigate this buddy system and send them to the magic carpet area. Let them share a sitting space to play their game.

Some folder games have one correct answer, such as matching objects. Others are open ended (there is more than one way of doing the activity). An example of this type of folder would be to attach a piece of write-and-wipe contact paper to the inside of a folder. Children can draw a picture or write the letters of the alphabet and then wipe it off and start over with a new idea. Have some folders encourage cooperative

play, such as a tic-tac-toe game. Laminate the page with the tic-tac-toe grid so children can write on it with crayon or water-based markers and wipe it off to begin a new game.

There are many excellent resource books on file folder games. Most include patterns and directions for making various games that enhance growth in many developmental areas.

Variations

Substitute manila envelopes for file folders. The activity surface is on the outside of the envelope. Store the pieces inside it.

Playing on the Wall

Materials/Preparation

* ⋆ An involvement activity bulletin board (directions on page 106)

Procedure

Involvement boards brighten up the room and, if they are put at the child's height, are great for an instant wait time activity. Children can work individually or cooperatively.

Involvement boards can teach many concepts. For example, place ten numbered nests on the board and have children put the correct number of eggs in them. Use story characters on another involvement board. Children can manipulate them to make up a new story or retell an old favorite. (Winnie the Pooh characters are an excellent example.)

It is best if the boards are self-explanatory, although sometimes you will need to give the children quick guidelines soon after you put up the display. Following brief and clear directions, children should be able to use the board without further supervision. Looped fabric with hooked fastener pieces are the easiest type of fasteners for children to use. Children feel good about their abilities as they master these involvement board skills.

Variations

Use a large flannel, magnetic, and looped fabric board as a portable involvement bulletin board. Set it on an easel and place it on the floor in your group area. Directions for making this type of board are on page 107; directions for making an easel start on page 93.

If you don't have a bulletin board at the child's level, cover a cardboard barrel with looped fabric and use it as a bulletin board-in-the-round. Directions are on page 107.

A Bowl of Dough All My Own

Materials/Preparation

* Small margarine tub of playdough

* Small piece of foam rubber place mat or linoleum about 9″ square

* Manipulating utensils, such as rolling pin (3/4″ dowel stick about 9″ long), plastic pizza cutter, tongue depressor, meatballer, garlic press, plastic eggs, plastic bottle caps, cookie cutters, margarine tub lids

* Gallon size reclosable plastic bag

* Dough resource books (see appendix A)

Procedure

Working with playdough is a calming and open-ended activity. Prepare four or five playdough kits and place all the supplies together in one kit. With everything together, children can set up, play with the playdough, and clean up on their own.

Put two or three manipulating utensils, a tub of playdough, and a manipulation mat in the plastic bag. Vary the items in each bag so children have some choices. Try some new utensils. Cookie cutters tend to be less open-ended than some of the other utensils listed above. Also, try different playdough recipes. They expose children to a variety of textures and colors.

Give directions on use of playdough kits and safety factors for utensils, prior to setting them out.

Develop playdough kits that are theme related. For example, in the fall put orange, green, brown, or sawdust dough in the containers. A unit on pizza could include pizza cutters, small circular cutting utensils, margarine tub lids, and a garlic press for shredded cheese.

Variations

Stenciling materials make another quick kit idea. Place a variety of stencils, paper, pencils, and markers in a reclosable plastic bag. Include a magic working space such as a piece of vinyl tablecloth. Make the stencils out of heavy poster board or plastic margarine tub lids (the latter are much more durable). Shape stencils are good for a shape theme and quite open-ended. Encourage children to create their own farm scene by providing animals and barn stencils.

Puzzle Put Togethers

Materials/Preparation

* Puzzles, either purchased or handmade (directions for handmade puzzles on pages 108–9)

Procedure

Puzzles are a valuable item to have in your classroom; have them available to children for many parts of the day—but especially when you have some children finishing group activities. Include puzzles in your magic carpet area so children can use wait time well.

Have many purchased puzzles available that vary in difficulty to meet the developmental abilities of all the children (manufacturers usually offer guidelines). If you have a group of three year olds, provide them with puzzles at two- to four-year-old levels because the group will have a range of skills and developmental levels.

You can make handmade puzzles at a low cost. Have children paint or draw pictures and cut them into puzzles. When children make their own puzzles, their interest increases.

Take photographs of the children and have them enlarged, or enlarge them on a copy machine, and cut them into a puzzle. Use calendar pictures or poster board wall decorations that relate to your theme to make into puzzles.

Puzzles are a quiet activity that challenge the children's developmental growth in many areas. With them, children work on their fine motor and eye-hand coordination and cognitive abilities. They develop social skills as they work together. Completing a puzzle enhances their self-esteem.

Variations

Provide large floor puzzles to encourage cooperative play. Make them out of picture posters or trace children's bodies onto heavy poster board. Have children color or paint them. Cover with clear contact paper and cut them into pieces. This will probably be one of the first magic carpet activities pulled off the shelf.

A Box of My Own

Materials/Preparation

* Individual felt boxes (directions on page 109)

Procedure

Children like to have ownership of something—something that is just theirs. Make this possible by providing a school box for each child in your group. If you want to economize and recycle, acquire shoe boxes from a shoe department or store instead of purchasing school boxes. Let the children decorate the outside of the box to make it even more personal.

Encourage children to get out a magic carpet and invite a friend to bring over their felt box. The partners might copy each other's patterns or share pieces.

Variations

Some alternatives to school or shoe boxes are cigar boxes, large margarine tubs, or lunch boxes. It is best to determine the amount of space you have available for storing these containers, before you purchase or begin collecting them. Also, be aware of where you are storing the boxes. Put them in a place where children can get and return them easily.

You and I Photo Books

Materials/Preparation

* A variety of handmade photo books (directions on pages 109–10)

Procedure

Children love looking at photographs of themselves and pictures they have drawn. Get children interested in books through this natural love. They will spend many minutes paging through the interesting photos and pictures placed in the book.

Take photographs of the children throughout the day at the center or when you take a field trip. Develop the pictures and place them in a durable book so the children can look at and recall the special events. Add to the book or exchange the pictures as you acquire more photos. Place the book with the other ones in the room, so children can freely choose it during magic carpet times.

Have each child make their own book and fill it with drawings of themselves, their house, their favorite animals, colors, and toys. Acquire photos from their parents also. Place all of the books on the shelf so the children can learn facts about their friends. It is a good opportunity to build children's self-esteem. This is definitely an enjoyable and calming magic carpet activity.

Variations

If you don't have time to make books, purchase small pocket-sized albums and place photos of the children in the pages. After the children have had ample time to look at these mini-albums, replace the old photos with new ones to renew their interest.

Page protectors (clear plastic covering for paper with holes punched) in three-ring binders also serve as handmade photo book pages.

Terrific Tin Activities

Materials/Preparation

* Tins

* Objects such as small plastic farm animals or dinosaurs, magnetic letters and numbers, a variety of counters and sorters, or beads for stringing

Procedure

Tins are a versatile and popular item; you can get them decorated with different scenes and designs. Look for a tin that has a farm or prehistoric scene on it, or one that has bears on it.

Have tins available on the magic carpet activity shelf for children to choose and manipulate the objects inside. Some excellent fillers are listed below.

* Small plastic animals with fences to build a farm scene and act out the role of the farmer or the animals.

* Small plastic dinosaurs to pretend they are living in prehistoric times. Children enjoy sorting them and stating facts about each type of dinosaur.

* Teddy bear counters (they come in small, medium, and large sizes) to sequence, develop patterns, count, and tell the story of "The Three Bears."

* Beads and strings to create necklaces and develop fine motor skills, patterning, and strengthen eye-hand coordination.

* Magnetic numbers and letters to build reading and math concepts. They also stick to the tin and its lid.

Be creative in thinking of other items to store in and use with a tin. However, we strongly suggest you include larger objects that cannot be swallowed or choked on, especially if you have children who still put nonedible items in their mouth.

If possible, correlate what is in the tins with the design on the outside. Children will be able to determine the content without opening the tin. If you don't find the tin design you want, purchase a solid colored tin and label it with words or stickers.

Variations

Substitute large margarine tubs or plastic whipped cream containers for tins. Use permanent markers for labeling.

Cooperating with the Cube

Materials/Preparation

* Looped fabric cube (directions on page 101)

* Symbols to go on the cube (made from foam rubber place mats, stiff pellon, etc.) with hooked fastener on back.

* Optional: box of items, including pom-poms (pages 96–97), beanbags (page 95), etc.

Procedure

The looped fabric cube has possibilities for cooperative play during those magic carpet times. Children take turns tossing and naming the symbol that lands on the cube. Place symbols on the cube that children are learning such as numerals, letters, colors, or shapes.

Put numerals on the cube. When the children toss it, they pull that number of pom-poms out of a box. Repeat. Now count or add up the number of pom-poms together. Substitute beanbags for pom-poms. Toss them into a bucket.

If the children are learning colors, put color symbols on the cube. When tossing the cube, they pull all of the pom-poms that are that color out of the box.

The cube keeps children meaningfully occupied, with all of its possibilities, for a long time. Encourage them to use their imagination to come up with their own ideas of play.

Variations

If you don't have a looped fabric cube, purchase a large sponge die (2″ to 4″). This is used in a smaller area than the cube and promotes smaller muscle control. The shared magic carpet is a perfect playing space for this activity. Have a bucket of cotton balls available. When the children roll the die, have them remove that number of cotton balls from the bucket with tongs. This activity also promotes math skills.

A Circle of Match-Ups

Materials/Preparation

* Matching Activity Board adapted from Lite Rite Folders in *Pocketful of Miracles—Holiday Folder Games* by Connie Eisenhart (Partner Press, 1985)

* Continuity tester (available at hardware or auto parts stores for $3 to $15)

* Circle of Match-Up game (directions on pages 110–11)

Procedure

Magic carpet activities should sustain the children's attention for approximately five to ten minutes. This game is certain to do that! Make several matching activity boards and have continuity testers available.

Children enjoy taking several of these circles to a magic carpet alone or with a friend. To make this a cooperative activity, two children each take one end of the continuity tester. One child places their end of the continuity tester in a punched hole near one picture. The other child finds the matching picture and places their end of the continuity tester in that punched hole. If they have made a match, the continuity tester lights up—and so do the children's faces. This is a self-reinforcing activity. Place several matching pictures on each circle because children become involved and motivated by this activity.

The match-ups are made by drawing pictures, adhering stickers, rubber stamping, or stenciling. Coordinate them with concepts and/or a theme. Although circles of match-ups using continuity testers takes a little extra time to make, it is well worth the effort.

When an individual child finishes their circle of match-ups, they can trade with their magic carpet friend and begin the fun all over again.

Variation

If you don't have the time or the materials to make and do circle of match-ups, the following variation is also self-correcting and easier to make.

Make your circle of match-ups without the holes and the aluminum foil strips connecting the holes. Have children make the matches by clipping a clothespin or spring clip on both pictures. On the back, make matching symbols, such as colored dots, directly behind the matching pictures. For example, use red dots on the back of the pig cards, blue dots for the cows, and so on. As children turn the circle over, if the clothespins are clipped to the matching symbol on the back, they have done it right. Remove the clothespins and make another match.

Let's Touch

Materials/Preparation

* Clear plastic bins or shoe boxes covered with patterned contact paper

* A set of manipulative items for each box or bin, such as all plastic items or all wooden items

Procedure

Prepare several let's touch bins or boxes that children can use individually or in groups of twos or threes. Fill them with materials that are of interest to children. Collect items and group them because of a common factor. Wooden items in one box might include clothespin, napkin rings, golf tees, dice, blocks, and wooden spoons. A bin with metal items might contain large nuts and bolts, a ruler, chain links, jewelry, stainless steel flatware, and magnets.

When you add a new box, introduce it to the children. Demonstrate some uses for the objects in the box and let the children use their imaginations and senses. Provide opportunities for counting, sorting, stacking, building, tossing, making patterns, and dramatic play. This activity is enjoyed by children of all ages.

In addition to preparing some of the boxes on your own or with the children, encourage parents to get involved. Send home a list of items that could be used in these let's touch boxes. Stress safety when selecting items; make sure items are free of rust, contain no sharp edges, and are not too small.

Variations

Some alternatives to bins or boxes are ice cream buckets, large resealable plastic bags, or two-pound margarine tubs.

Buddy Buckets

Materials/Preparation

* Buddy Buckets (directions on pages 111–112)
* Handmade game or manipulatives for two children
* Dog and Bones game (page 112)

Procedure

Buddy Buckets are activities designed for two children. Choose games or manipulatives that encourage and promote cooperative play. Prepare several buckets and store them so children can get, use, and return them without your assistance. In each bucket, include a square of material, or a towel and a game, or a cooperative toy. Children use the square of material or towel to sit on or for their play materials.

One buddy bucket might contain a number concept game called Dog and Bones. The game includes a dog cutout or a small stuffed dog, actual dog treats that come in different shapes, a plastic dish, and number/shape cards. Children play the game by drawing a number/shape card and feeding the dog the appropriate number of shaped pieces. Children take turns and can help each other. Another bucket might contain a homemade game board, die, and playing pieces.

Children can choose their partner, but there may be times when you wish to pair a particular child with another. For example, pair a child who understands number concepts with a child whose number concepts are just emerging. These two children will complement each other.

Variation

If you don't have time to make the games for the buddy buckets, use manipulatives from your shelf. Manipulatives that promote turn taking and cooperation include dominoes, floor puzzles, matching sound cylinders, and pattern-matching games.

Magnificent Magnetic Wands

Materials/Preparation

* Magnetic wand
* Metal or magnetic objects
* Poster board path for object to follow

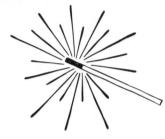

(directions for magnetic wands, objects, and path on pages 112–113)

* Pom-pom pals (page 102)

Procedure

Magnetic wands are a different kind of wand from what we've discussed previously in this book, but they are no less magical. These wands are perfect for a magic carpet activity.

Draw a path on a piece of poster board. Place an object with a metal or magnetic base on top of the poster board. Pom-pom pals, with a tack glued into the bottom of them, work great for this activity. They have a steady base and are lightweight. Move the magnetic wand under the poster board path until it contacts the tack or magnet at the bottom of the object. The object will stick to the wand through the poster board and move with it. Watch as it treks, twists, and twirls along the path.

Vary the complexity of the activity depending on the abilities of your children. Make some open-ended paths and others that have a beginning and ending point. Typically, this activity is played individually, but children can also play together sharing and switching paths. It requires few pieces that are easily kept together in a reclosable gallon size plastic bag or manila envelope. It requires concentration, so it tends to be a quiet and calming activity.

Purchase or make several magnetic wands because this is sure to be a favorite. Or simply use a magnetic disk.

Variations

Here's another fun magnet activity. Take a twenty-ounce clear plastic pop bottle and remove the outside sticker. (If you are having difficulty doing this, rub nail polish remover over the sticky residue.) Fill the bottle about half full with dry baby cereal, salt, or sand. Drop metal objects, such as nails, bolts, nuts, metal rimmed bingo chips, paper clips, or metal shavings into the bottle. Cap the bottle and wrap duct tape around the cap and neck so children cannot get it open. Rub the magnetic wand over the sides of the bottle and watch the objects being pulled to the surface of the bottle.

Children will be mesmerized—magnetic wands are truly magical and magnificent!

To Get Started:

Create special games and activities stored in a special magical place for those difficult "waiting" times.

Magical Moments

Children in the school district's early childhood classroom were often out of the room. Mrs. Samuels and Mr. Mark took them to their therapies, out to the bus, and down the hall and around the corner to wash hands, toilet, and diaper. Many times when they are on the move they have to wait. One day, while diapering Tekia, Mrs. Samuels turned around and saw Chuck and Shaba wildly splashing water in the sink. She heard Connie and Ying running up and down the hall. Mr. Mark was tending to Shannon whose brace needed adjusting. Mrs. Samuels sighed a huge sigh. "When I win the lottery, I'm going to have a fully equipped adaptive classroom!"

How can Mrs. Samuels and Mr. Mark help children through these out-of-the-classroom waiting times that simply are unavoidable?

First, they can anticipate and plan for those on-the-move waiting times. Second, they can turn those wait times into magical moments by taking a small portable bag of tricks with them when they take the children to the bus or down the hall. Fill your bag of tricks with activity ideas from this chapter.

Guidelines

1. Look at your schedule again and continue to eliminate children's waiting time when possible. Use the worksheet in part 1 to help you.

2. Use the Triple A strategy. Anticipate and avert wait time problems by looking ahead. Act by bringing simple items with you when you go to the bathroom down the hall. Place small items, such as a kazoo or a glove puppet, in your pocket for later use.

3. Look at your immediate surroundings for ideas to help children wait. Ask children to look at clouds and describe what they see. Use games such as, "I Think I See" or "I See Someone Wearing."

4. Sing songs or finger plays that the children suggest. Commit them to memory.

5. Develop your personal portable bag of tricks. Include a variety of small props for on-the-go, have-to-wait moments. Use these when you have no choice but to wait with small children.

The ideas in this chapter are especially appropriate when you are on the move with children. However, use these ideas for any transition time during your day.

Activities

Pocket Apron

Materials/Preparation

* Purchase a bib style apron or make your own apron (three to six pockets); directions for the apron (variation 1) on pages 99–100

Procedure

Become a person of mystery by wearing an apron with pockets stuffed full of small interesting objects. Tuck a tiny fuzzy animal, a beautiful rock or crystal, finger puppets, a tiny music box, pipe cleaners, or other small items into the apron pockets prior to wearing it with the children. Now you are prepared and ready for action. Wear the multi-pocketed apron on field trips, while walking to the store, when greeting children at the bus, or wherever you want to share a magical moment with children.

The surprises you bring engage children in the fun. On a field trip to an apple orchard, pull out two tiny red fabric apples and do an apple finger play. When visiting a planetarium, hide glow-in-the-dark stars in the apron's pockets. Give each child one of the stars to wear and glow, while singing, "Twinkle, Twinkle, Little Star." On a snowy day, pull out small inexpensive plastic magnifying glasses, one for each child, and take the children outdoors to investigate the flakes. Change the hidden items frequently and continue to surprise and motivate the children.

Variations

Sew pockets of various sizes, shapes, and fabrics. Fill with creative fun!

Picture This

Materials/Preparation

* Pictures or stickers of items to initiate songs and finger plays
* Mount everything on colored note cards

Procedure

We successfully avert problems while on a field trip, a walk to the store, or a visit to the park by anticipating the needs of children. We all know how difficult it is to sit quietly and still for a long time.

Carry some small note cards with stickers or pictures in your pocket or in a small bag. Use these to motivate children to sing songs, recite poems, or do finger plays. Some of our favorite visual aids are a picture of a steamy bowl of porridge to encourage the spontaneous telling of the adventures of "The Three Bears" or a photograph of a farm couple, which encourages songs like "The Farmer in the Dell" and "Old MacDonald." A drawing of bananas provides the opportunity to sing "Five Little Monkeys" or "Apples and Bananas." These pictorial cues enable children to remember many songs and finger plays.

Name That Tune!

Materials/Preparation

* Kazoo

Procedure

Reach into your pocket, a basket, a bag, or wherever you keep special magical items and pull out a kazoo. Use the kazoo to play a familiar song and have the

children hum as you repeat the tune. Next, ask them to name the tune. Sing the words of the familiar songs after the title has been established.

Make the moment special by adding new words or movements to the melody. For example, use the melody from "The Farmer in the Dell" and sing about the field trip the group is experiencing.

We're waiting for the bus. We're waiting for the bus.

Hi Ho the Derry O. We're waiting for the bus.

We're on our way to the forest. We're on our way to the forest.

Hi Ho the Derry O. We're on our way to the forest.

We're going to see some trees. We're going to see some trees.

Hi Ho the Derry O. We're going to see some trees.

One more block to go. One more block to go.

Hi Ho the Derry O. One more block to go.

Other rousing familiar songs include, "Miss Mary Mack," "Do You Know the Muffin Man?," "Happy Birthday," and "Old MacDonald." This portable activity works especially well on a walk, field trip, outside, or anywhere one is apt to burst into song. Promote listening skills, the ability to match rhythm and tune as well as enjoying the moment!

Variations

Omit the kazoo and hum a favorite song for the children to match and guess the title.

Act It Out

Materials/Preparation

* Storytelling mitten (directions page 114)
* Pom-pom pals (directions page 102)

Procedure

This magical moment can occur whenever you and the children are on the move. Attach simple and portable pom-pom pal characters to the storytelling mitten. Bring the mitten with you when you take the children somewhere in the building or on outings. It changes unproductive waiting time into productive enjoyable moments.

Encourage singing songs and finger plays or acting out creative story lines. For example, on a bus trip to a local farm, bring out the mitten and share the attached animals as you travel. A cow character prompts children to sing "Did You Feed My Cow?," "The Farmer in the Dell," or "Old MacDonald," among others.

In a park setting, share the mitten with the children using a squirrel or bird character. These pom-pom pals suggest the song, "Gray Squirrel, Gray Squirrel" or the finger play, "Two Little Blackbirds."

Variations

Give the children animal or people finger puppets to challenge their creative abilities. Make paper headbands for the children that initiate stories, songs, finger plays, etc. Some headband picture ideas include lambs for "Mary Had a Little Lamb" or "Baa, Baa, Black Sheep" or spiders to prompt "Eency, Weency Spider" or "Little Miss Muffet." Use stickers, drawings, and rubber stamps to illustrate.

Object Hunt

Materials/Preparation

* Mount a variety of colored shapes on poster board cards (8″ x 10″). Cover with clear contact paper.

Procedure

Encourage the natural curiosity of children whenever and wherever the occasion arises. Pass time in a positive manner and reinforce color and shape recognition skills in the children. Show the children a card that has a pictorial representation of a particular shape and color. Then ask the group to find items in the environment that would match the shape or color or both. For example, show a card with a green rectangle to the boys and girls while walking down a hall for a bathroom routine. This prompts them to look around and find a green door, a green table in the hall, and green roof on the building across the street.

While on a field trip to a restaurant, display a card with a white circle. The children spot a clock with a white face, a sign hanging in the restaurant, or a tortilla on a plate. This activity can be done both indoors and outdoors. Repeat it often throughout the day and note how the children improve their powers of observation.

Variation

Choose an object in the environment and name all the colors and shapes seen in it. For example, walk with the children outside your building. Look at a house in the neighborhood and name colors and shapes such as a red rectangle—door, a black triangle—window, and a green square—lawn.

Ribbons and Rings

Materials/Preparation

* Ribbons and Rings (directions page 114)

Procedure

Sometimes we just have to wait with children. The bus is late or the other classroom is late getting out of the playroom. Use ribbons and rings (bracelets) for those wait times. Prepare enough bracelets for each child; for yourself, prepare a master ring (bracelet) that has all the colors of ribbons.

If you have to wait down the hall or outside, take this portable activity with you and give one ribbon and ring to each child. While you're waiting, ask questions such as, "Show me if you have red, show me if you have blue." If children need prompting, use your ring of colored ribbons. Give children directional statements using the colors. For example, "If you have a pink ring, hold it up in the air. If you have yellow stand up." For older preschoolers, make it more challenging by giving two to three directions at one time to test their recall. "If you have a purple ring, tap your head, wiggle your fingers, and blink your eye." Use the rings to dismiss the children by color or as a ticket they put back into the bucket before they get on the bus. As in any activity, it is important to supervise. It is tempting for some children to put the colorful ribbons into their mouth.

Variations

The ribbons and rings work successfully for stretching activities, too. Provide each child with a ring. Using almost any type of musical tape, have children move to the rhythm. These colorful ribbons are great motivators. They work especially well for movement activities because children can put them on their wrist, allowing them to use both hands for clapping.

Peek Hole Folder Games

Materials/Preparations

★ Peek hole folders (directions on pages 114–15)

Procedure

Share a magical moment with children indoors or outdoors, whenever time permits. Take several peek hole folders along for the bus ride on a field trip. Show one of the folders to a small group of children or an individual. Ask them to focus on what they see through the peek holes. Foster the guessing process as they look at the peek holes and try to determine what object or picture is hidden. Use thoughtful and creative questions and offer some hints and clues as needed.

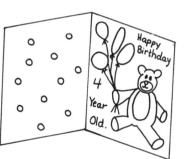

One special clue is a short poem that goes with the object that you attach to the inside flap of the folder. Read this to the children as they attempt to guess the object in the peek hole. Even after the boys and girls know what the surprise is, they can continue this activity. They will find it fun to trick their friends and give the hints as they were given to them.

Continue to add to your collection of peek hole folders. The children enjoy making them, also.

Variations

Used greeting cards make quick and interesting peek hole games. Fold the card the opposite way and punch one or more holes in strategic locations.

Bubbles on a Rope

Materials/Preparations

★ Purchase a small bottle of bubble solution attached to a cord (refillable)

Procedure

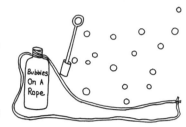

Outside in the sunshine or in the room, open the magical bottle and gently blow some of the bubbles. Because the wand is small, the bubbles will be tiny. Children and adults find magic in tiny bubbles to scatter, track, catch, and enjoy. Do this fun activity while waiting for a school bus, on a field trip, taking a walk in the park, or anytime you want to share the experience.

Variations

If you live in a climate that has cold winter weather, try blowing bubbles in the air outdoors on a cold day when the temperature is 10 degrees Fahrenheit or colder. Blow the bubbles and watch them become frosty and freeze in midair. Slowly, they will fall to the ground and shatter. You will want to be outside for only a brief time, but the spectacle of tiny bubbles floating, freezing in the air, and falling to the ground and shattering is worth the trip.

Stomp, Clap, Clap, Tap

Materials/Preparations

★ No materials required

Procedure

Look into your bag of tricks and help children find magic in the movement of their bodies. No matter what the surroundings—a field trip, walking down the halls, or a bus ride home—we can help children in self-discovery and enhance the moment.

Show boys and girls how to use their hands, feet, arms, and other body parts to create rhythmic patterns. As they duplicate the clapping and tapping you do, they improve their listening skills along with interpreting the sounds and making movements.

Clap or tap a simple pattern starting with two to three actions and progressing to more complex patterns. Try the following clapping with hands, tapping with toes, stomping with feet, rubbing hands, and snapping fingers. Some simple patterns are listed below.

Clap   Clap, Clap   Tap   Tap, Tap

Tap, Tap, Rub   Tap, Tap, Rub

Stomp, Stomp, Stomp   Stomp Tap, Tap

Snap   Clap, Clap   Snap   Clap, Clap

Here are more complex patterns:

Clap, Tap, Stomp, Stomp, Stomp
Clap, Tap, Stomp, Stomp, Stomp

Tap, Tap, Rub   Tap, Tap, Rub
Tap, Rub, Tap, Rub, Tap, Tap, Tap

Snap, Stomp, Tap   Snap, Stomp, Tap
Snap, Snap, Stomp, Stomp, Tap

Vary the beat, speed, and patterns so the children are able to do the actions successfully. Happy clapping!

Folding Wand

Materials/Preparations

* Folding wand (directions on page 90)

Procedure

Magical moments are sure to occur when you use this folding wand as a portable prop. Rather than always asking young children to stand still, move quietly, or walk in the line, encourage a variety of exciting and creative ways to move them from one place to another.

Pull out your convenient wand and help children imagine that they are an animal. Direct them to move in an appropriate manner for that creature. Say to them, "If you were a tiny mouse, you might hide among the rocks. Think about how you could make yourself very small." Tap the children gently with the folding wand and watch them move.

As children wait in line for lunch, direct them to move like a dinosaur hunting for food in the woods or a hungry fish swimming through the water in search of food. Allow the children to show how they would move in that manner. Wave the wand over the group of children to start and stop the movements.

Items in your environment can help you and the children imagine various creatures. If you are on a walk, you might spot a squirrel, rabbit, dog, ant, and butterfly to imitate. A field trip to a farm, zoo, or park will offer still more ideas.

Variations

In addition to animals, imitate people. Try to walk like toddlers, football players, or someone carrying a bag of groceries.

If you are leaving the center, bring action pictures in a bag. Direct children to look at the pictures for movement ideas.

I See Someone Wearing

Materials/Preparations

* No materials required

Procedure

Magical moments happen anytime and anyplace when we give children positive recognition and attention. We avoid potential behavior problems by catching them being good.

Take time to notice what an individual or small group of children is wearing each day. For example, you notice that John, a rather active boy, is wearing new tennis shoes. Tell him, "Those new shoes with racing stripes have a lot of bounce. I saw you running very quickly outside today." In addition to giving him some positive attention, you have reminded him that running is one of the things we do outside. Encourage him to share your description of his new shoes with his friends. This promotes his language skills, and helps him feel good about himself.

For your comments, you can choose unique items, such as glitter T-shirts, long zippers, hair ribbons, turtleneck shirts, character shirts, and handmade items. Do this while in a group and ask a particular child to stand up so the other children are able to see. With your descriptions, you will add a variety of new words to their vocabulary. Caution: Avoid overuse of this technique or too much emphasis on clothing. Rather, stress uniqueness of each child.

Variations

Ask the children to observe you or another adult in the environment. Highlight some special piece of clothing. You might wear some interesting jewelry, such as animal earrings or fruit pins, that would promote descriptive words or initiate a song. For example, fish earrings would prompt the children to sing "1, 2, 3, 4, 5…I caught a fish alive."

Follow the Singing Leader

Materials/Preparations

* **No materials required**

Procedure

This magical moment is simple to do anyplace. Start with several follow the leader actions, encouraging children to listen and watch carefully. Then try this variation of follow the leader—and be a singing leader.

As a singing leader, sing the first four lines of a familiar song. Ask children to repeat those four lines (add actions as appropriate). Start with "Eency Weency Spider," "Where is Thumbkin?," "If You're Happy and You Know It," and other familiar tunes. Remember to include songs that you taught the children earlier in the year. (Sometimes we get involved with new songs and forget to enjoy the past favorites, too.)

After the children follow you as the singing leader, ask for a volunteer to lead the group. Suggest a song or let the leader choose one. This boosts self-esteem and self-discipline as children use their time in a way they love, singing!

Variations

Sing familiar songs with a variety of emotions for an unusual experience. Try "Twinkle, Twinkle, Little Star" while crying or "Did You Feed My Cow?" while laughing, then crying. See song books in appendix A.

I Think I See

Materials/Preparations

* **No materials required**

Procedure

Field trips provide us with new and stimulating environments. Encourage children to observe and describe what they see. Help children focus on a particular item. While walking to the store on a lovely spring day, one teacher and her children stopped at a corner for a red light. The teacher said, "I think I see a car with a missing roof. Look, it's a dark blue car, a _____! (convertible) Who do you see driving the car?"

In another case, at a local fresh produce market, say, "Boys and girls, I think I see that man in the tan suit buying a special fruit. It is shaped like a very large egg, has a dark green skin and is very tasty! I think I see a _____." (watermelon) Children become aware of their surroundings as you share these magical moments with them.

Variations

Ask children to use their imagination and think what might be in the environment. For example, as you spend time in a park, one child says, "I think I see an animal that likes to hide nuts for the winter." The other children will guess the animal is a squirrel and then look for one, too.

All Right, Puffs of White!

Materials/Preparations

* **No materials required**

Procedure

Take some time to reflect on cloud formations while taking a walk or waiting for a bus. Ask children to lie on their backs and observe the sky. Naturally, someone might say the clouds look like cotton candy. Encourage them to watch and think some more. Talk about and describe what is seen in the clouds.

On one windy day, when dark clouds moved as a group of children watched, one child described this cloud picture as "a big black cat sneaking up on the two silly mice."

Point out the twists, turns, and swirls as children watch the clouds. Some clouds look like mountains with snow and then the snow moves and seems to melt. Others remind you of animals, people, characters, familiar objects, and strange creatures.

Enjoy! You might even be fortunate enough to see a rainbow.

Variations

* Give children chalk for sidewalk art after viewing the clouds.

* Give each child a portable pinhole viewer. This allows the child to focus on a small portion of a tree, flower, or the sky.

* Take pieces of string or cording material about 1 yard long and tie them into circles. Give each child a circle to spread on the lawn, sidewalk, or by a tree. Ask them to search and describe what they find in their circles, including tiny insects, bits of sand, litter, and flowers. What a different view of the world!

Photo Mania

Materials/Preparation

* Large magazine picture or greeting card collages.

* Mount pictures on poster board and cover with clear contact paper.

Procedure

Create a magical moment as children engage in such routine tasks as toileting, hand washing, and getting a drink. Hang one of your collage creations in the bathroom area, next to the drinking fountain, or wherever children need to wait their turn. Choose a theme for the collage and hide an unusual character like a teddy bear or an object such as the American flag several times throughout the collage.

Direct the boys and girls to view the poster many times throughout the day in order to find the special people, characters, or objects. By anticipating that waiting during a routine may create a problem, you have averted trouble.

Children of all ages will enjoy the challenge of finding the hidden items. Some concentrate individually, others like to work cooperatively and share the surprises. Change the collage posters frequently (about once a week) and repeat some as the year progresses.

Variations

Use photographs of the children to create a collage of your group engaged in a variety of activities.

To Get Started:

Take a bag of tricks with you when you are on the move with children.

You're Excused

Children in the All Out of Time Day Care couldn't wait for outdoor play. They loved the challenge of racing their friends to be the first in line. Today Ms. Vue gave the direction, "Let's all line up at the door." As a result, all twenty children ran to the door at once. "Wait a minute" didn't stop the children. At the door, there was some pushing and jockeying for position in line. One child came up to Ms. Vue and cried, "Audra pushed me. I was first in line and she pushed me." Ms. Vue thought, "There has to be a better way!"

What could she have done to avoid the hassle at the door? Is there something she could have done to make excusing the children a smoother and more enjoyable transition?

Excusing children seems like a simple process, but like all other transitions we need to anticipate and plan for it. Children are very literal, thus they take you at your word. Therefore, give directions carefully. Ms. Vue needs to think through her method of excusing and choose her words carefully in order to avoid chaos. This chapter includes special activities and visual aids to guide children through the excusing process.

Guidelines

1. Plan how you will excuse the children.

2. Avoid open-ended directions, such as "We can all go out to play now."

3. Explain what will happen next in steps. For example, "First Jenny will tap you with the magic wand. Then you can go to the cubby to get your jacket." Use one-step, two-step, or three-step directions appropriate for the age of the children.

4. Use a tangible object to focus children's attention on the move they have to make. Puppets are great motivators.

5. Use a combination of the guidelines to smooth your daily transitions. For example, use a puppet to give two-step and three-step directions to children.

6. Position one staff member to receive the children as they are excused.

7. Change the pace of excusing children. Sometimes it's best if one child at a time leaves the group. Sometimes it's all right for a few or half the group to go together.

8. Positively reinforce children who are leaving group appropriately.

Activities

A Tip for a Tap

Materials/Preparations

* No materials required
* Optional: a wand, prop, or other visual (directions for felt bell wand on page 88)

Procedure

Children eagerly await the individual recognition you give by tapping them as a cue to be excused. Often it's beneficial to excuse them one at a time. Tap their heads, shoulders, folded hands, or other parts of their body to regulate the pace as they move to the next area or activity. Use a faithful wand or any other prop you shared during group time. A felt bell wand with small jingle bells sewn onto it makes a quiet tinkling sound as children leave the group. Choose a child to do the tapping for a change of pace. If no props are available, give gentle taps with your hand. As you excuse the children, sing a song, give them a personalized good-bye or directions on where they should go next.

Variations

Try a "traveling tap." You tap one child, that child taps another child and so on until all children are excused.

Wiggle Worms

Materials/Preparations

* One or two chairs that children can wiggle and squirm under; or a barrel (an open cylinder) or box they can climb through

Procedure

Oh, what fun children have as they wiggle away from group time. This is a good activity to excuse one or two children at a time. Sing the following song to the same tune as the first four lines of "Turkey In The Straw":

Oh, he wiggled and he squirmed and he looked just like a worm.

Oh, he wiggled and he squirmed and he looked just like a worm.

Oh, he wiggled and he squirmed and he looked just like a worm.

There goes (child's name) right on through.

As you sing the child's name, they go to the chair, barrel, or box, get down on their tummies and crawl through or under the equipment. Set up two separate chairs, barrels, or boxes, as it takes longer for some children to complete the task. Position  the items so they point toward the area you want them to go.

Sometimes you'll get a child who doesn't feel comfortable crawling under the chair, barrel, or box. Encourage them, but don't force. Remember to rein-

force children appropriately wiggling their bodies right into the next activity.

Variations

Another song for the same type of excusing is sung to the first two lines of "Old MacDonald Had a Farm."

Wiggle (child's name) like a worm.

Right under the chair. (or through the barrel or box)

Jack or Jill in the Box

Materials/Preparations

* No materials required

Procedure

The finger play "Jack in the Box" is one of the children's favorites. Because of its popularity, adapt it to an excusing activity. Have all of the children squat down as if they were in a box. While they are preparing themselves or before you start excusing, remember to tell children where they're going and what they'll be doing. "You'll be going to the sink to wash your hands. Then to the lunch table." Chant the finger play, replacing "Jack" with children's names. It goes like this:

(child's name) in the box sits so still,

Will you come out?

And the child jumps up and responds:

Yes I will!

That child leaves the group and moves to the next activity.

When you have another teacher or assistant participating in group time, excuse them first to model for the children and move to the next area. In this case, go to the sink. This is especially important because it takes a little longer to excuse children this way. The other adult is positioned at the new activity to guide children. Repeat the finger play until everyone has jumped out of their imaginary box. After some of the

group is gone, ask another child to recall the transition they are making. Ask a child who benefits from reminders.

Variations

For a little variety, change the level of your voice. One time speak loudly and another time whisper it, depending on the mood of the children and/or the mood you want to set. Whisper to quiet them after a particularly active group time.

The Name Game

Materials/Preparations

* **No materials required**

Procedure

Visibly showing children where they are to go quickens the transition. Excuse yourself first for this game. Position yourself at or near the destination area. If children are to go to lunch, stand near the table and excuse them, stating their name.

If your first name is (child's first name) ,

If your last name is (child's last name) ,

If your name is (child's first and last names) .

As children get older, they become intrigued with first, last and full names. Sing this song to the tune "Happy Birthday."

If your name is (child's first and last names) ,

If your name is (child's first and last names) ,

If your name is (child's first and last names) ,

You may go to (state where they are to move to).

Variations

Put letters on a felt board and say, "If your name begins with this letter, you are excused," or "If your name has this letter in it, you are excused." Also, sign the letters using American Sign Language to expose children to other communication practices. (Sign language resource books are in appendix A.)

Another option is to verbally spell the children's names or use the felt letters to spell them. Do this activity with children who recognize their written name.

Critical Thinking

Materials/Preparations

* **No materials required**

Procedure

Moving children from one activity to another can be an event. Direct children to move in interesting ways and also help them develop critical thinking skills. Make use of open-ended and varied questions to encourage the children to put their minds in gear. Ask the children, "If you could not use your feet, how would you get to the cubbies and go outside?" When children offer suggestions, direct them to move to the cubbies. Some children roll, others crawl. Help children stretch their imagination. It is important to reinforce their correct or appropriate responses.

Plan other things to say to excuse the children. Ask, "If you had three legs, how would you move? Show me. Pretend your legs are glued together and will not come apart. Show me how you will get to the art table." After children have had practice with this, they are ready to offer their own suggestions.

Variations

Describe an object with a riddle and direct children to use other types of movements. "Think of a large animal with a trunk and huge ears. Move like that animal." Ask, "What has four legs and cannot walk? A chair! Pretend you are sitting on one and move to the next activity."

Puppets

Materials/Preparations

* **Puppet (hand, stick, finger, or body) either purchased or handmade**

Procedure

Introduce puppets, each with a distinctive personality, at group time. These puppets take on an active role, such as singing, leading a song, choosing a child to do a task, or laughing at the teacher's comments. For example, have the puppet say, "I choose Danny to get the balls for outside play."

When it is time to excuse the children, use the character again. As the puppet holds the interest of the children, it says names, taps, physically guides, or points to excuse children. Children respond and leave the group as others eagerly await their turn and receive individual recognition.

Variations

Allow one or more children to use a puppet and dismiss the children. Encourage the children to hug the puppet good-bye as they leave the group. This helps to teach appropriate social behaviors.

Machines and Tools

Materials/Preparations

* Actual machines and tools or use drawings, photos, or pictures of machines and tools

* Mount photos or pictures on 8″ x 10″ poster board and cover with clear contact paper

Procedure

Tell the children about a special way to excuse them from the group. Show a machine or tool. Discuss how it works and the action or movement it makes. Then, as you excuse the children, ask them to move by imitating the action of a particular machine or tool. Accept their efforts and reinforce the actions with appropriate comments. For example, show a picture of a washing machine and talk about the agitator and spin dry actions. Say to the children, "Pretend you are a washing machine. Move to the art area when I push your on button." Touch each child gently and activate the machine.

At times, the actual machine or tool is handy and easy to share. This offers real hands-on learning. In another case, demonstrate how scissors cut paper and cloth. Then ask children to think about making their bodies do what a scissors does. Some might suggest that their arms could be the blades. Other children might think that one's legs do that action. Direct the children to decide which way they want their scissors to move and to do just that when excused.

The following example works along with another technique. Say, "If you are three years old, move like a lawn mower. If you are four years old, move like a pair of scissors. If you have brown hair, pretend you are a hammer and pound the floor as you move to the playground."

Variations

Show children a picture of a tool or machine that they may not know, such as a printing press or table saw. Encourage them to imagine how the tool or machine works. Ask them to move in that manner.

Name Rhyming

Materials/Preparations

* No materials required

* Optional: prepare a list of the children's names with rhyming words

Procedure

Excuse children as you ask them to listen to words that rhyme with their names and to go to the next activity when they do. "If your name rhymes with berry, you may go to the lunch table." Larry, Carrie, and Mary will leave the group in an orderly manner. To reinforce the rhyme, repeat the child's name aloud as he or she leaves the group, "Larry, Carrie, and Mary rhyme with berry!"

Caution children to listen carefully. Proceed to the next word. If children have trouble hearing the rhyming sounds, repeat the word and say some names that rhyme. For example, "If your name sounds like penny, get your coats and prepare for a walk. Denny, Kenny, and Jenny may leave." Some unusual names may test your creativity. Be sure to include names that reflect ethnic diversity.

Closing with Clothes

Materials/Preparations

* No materials required
* Optional: visuals of different clothes (types, patterns, or colors)

Procedure

Take a close look at your clothes. This is a good activity for children to examine themselves and what they are wearing. Excuse the children by types of clothing; shoes (buckle, tie, tennis); shirts (stripes, polka dots, long sleeve); shorts; socks; and so on. If the children are young use visual aids to show them the different patterns or types of clothing.

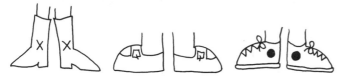

Refer to colors the children are wearing. At times, it is helpful for small groups of children to leave the area together. Then choose more unusual colors first, like purple or green. If you want several children to go at once, begin with blue, black, or white.

Following is a song for this type of dismissal. It's to the tune of "Row, Row, Row Your Boat."

Look, look, look around. Look around the room.

I see someone who's wearing (name a color or pattern).

You may be excused.

Before singing, remind children of any tasks they are to carry out, such as putting away their sitting spaces or taking off their name tags.

Variations

Here's another song to the tune of "Mary Had A Little Lamb."

I see a boy/girl who's wearing (name a color or pattern).

wearing (repeat item), wearing (repeat item).

I see a boy/girl who's wearing (repeat item).

You may be excused.

If you are excusing by colors, start with ones that relate to the theme, such as fall, spring, or patriotic colors.

Walk with the Animals

Materials/Preparations

* Drawings, pictures, and photos of animals
* Mount on 8" x 10" poster board and cover with clear contact paper

Procedure

When it's time to excuse children from group time to another activity, use animal pictures as visual aids. Encourage children to think about the animal depicted and how it moves and the sound it makes. As the group describes the movement of the animal, the children add new words to their vocabulary such as stalk, creep, crawl, and jump.

Have your set of animal cards ready. Ask one child to choose an animal card and show it to the group. When a child picks a card that shows a canary, ask their ideas on how birds move. Discuss their ideas of flying and hopping. Also, have them initiate the sounds birds make. Soon you will see children flapping their arms and hear their chirping sounds. Dismiss the birds alone or in pairs.

Other examples include strut and crow like a peacock, prowl like a cat, trot and neigh like a horse. Use animal and bird visual aids that are within your group's experience in order for them to imitate and relate to the experience.

Variations

Ask children wearing the color of the animal shown to move like that animal. When a brown earthworm is shown, those with brown skirts are excused first. Those wearing brown shoes are next. Continue with brown eyes, hair, socks, a shirt, and so on.

A Look at You

Materials/Preparations

★ No materials required

Procedure

"I am special. There's no one like me." These are the messages conveyed to children in this activity. Dismiss children by stating various body features. Some examples include hair, eyes, or skin color; freckles; glasses; short or long hair; or missing teeth. Here is a song that goes with this activity to the tune of "The Farmer in the Dell."

I see someone with (name a body feature).

I see someone with (repeat feature).

You may be excused.

I see someone with (repeat feature).

Focus on very unique characteristics so children truly can see how they are special.

Variations

Extend this activity by making poster board or stiff pellon features and placing them on a looped fabric cube (directions on page 101). Have a child roll the cube. Whatever the cube lands on (for example, brown hair), sing the song using that feature. Children with brown hair will leave. Repeat until all the children are excused. Make sure you have at least one feature characteristic of each child placed on the cube.

We Like You!

Materials/Preparations

★ No materials required

★ Optional: a waving hand wand (directions on page 89)

Procedure

This dismissal song leaves children with a positive self-concept. Either sing it or combine the song with a waving hand wand. Direct the wand at a particular child as you sing their name. The song is to the tune "Where Is Thumbkin?"

Good-bye (child's name) .

Good-bye (child's name) ,

We like you. Yes we do.

Good-bye (child's name) .

Good-bye (child's name) ,

We like you. Yes we do.

Sing one child's name or two or four through the whole song, depending on how quickly you want them to leave group. If you want the children to leave very quickly, sing "Good-bye (child's name) ." through the whole song. Omit the phrase "We like you. Yes we do." Sing a different child's name each time. Now eight children leave with just one verse of the song.

As you sing a child's name, they will move to the next activity you've prepared them for.

Variations

Have children pass the wand to each other as you sing the song. As they hand the wand to a friend, change the name to fit that child.

Gleeful Good-byes

Materials/Preparations

★ No materials required

Procedure

You've heard the following tune throughout the book. Use it one more time to say good-bye to children. Sing gleefully so children truly know you enjoyed having them in your group.

To excuse children slowly, repeat the same name throughout the complete song. If you want many children to go quickly, sing four different names throughout the song. As you sing the children's names, they leave the group and proceed to the next activity.

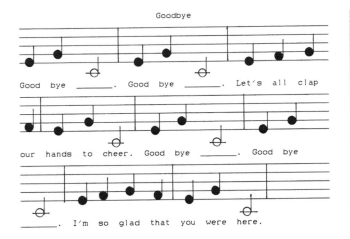

Goodbye

Good bye _____. Good bye _____. Let's all clap

our hands to cheer. Good bye _____. Good bye

_____. I'm so glad that you were here.

Variations

Here is another hearty good-bye sung to the tune of "Goodnight Ladies."

Good-bye (child's name) , good-bye (child's name) ,

Good-bye (child's name) .

I'm glad that you were here.

I Wand to be Excused

Materials/Preparations

★ Basic wand (directions on pages 86–7)

Procedure

Send children on to the next activity in a pleasant manner. Wave the magical wand over a child's head and chant: Ibbity Bibbity Boo, a ____ is just like you!"

Fill in the word you want the children to move like to the next activity. For example, mouse, kangaroo, frog, fairy, twinkling star, or floating leaf.

Reinforce their appropriate movements as they go. Usually, they are so busy concentrating on how they are moving they go to the next activity easily.

After the last child has been excused, follow the group to the next area. Physically guide any stragglers by placing your hand on their shoulders or taking their hand. Make that last contact during group time an enjoyable experience so children want to return.

Variations

Use the wand to tap the child's shoulder this time, and chant: "Ibbity Bibbity Boo, (spell child's name) can go, too!"

Do this with children who are skilled in spelling or hearing their names spelled. It is good for them to hear this and they are quite able to identify it.

Write the children's names on a dry erase board with a dry erase marker. Wipe off with tissue. Some three year olds can even visually identify their names.

To Get Started:

Excuse children by using interesting visuals and techniques.

Appendix

A

Teacher Resources

Records and Tapes

Bueffel, Elaine, and Carol Hammett: *Ball, Hoop and Ribbon Activities, It's Toddler Time*

Glass, Henry "Buzz," and Jack Capon: *Streamers and Ribbon Activities*

Greg and Steve: *We All Live Together*, Volumes I, II, III, IV, *Kids in Motion*

Hallum, Rosemary, Ph.D.: *Finger Play Fun*

Hallum, Rosemary, Ph.D., and Henry "Buzz" Glass: *Finger Plays and Footplays*

Jenkins, Ella: *And One and Two, You'll Sing a Song and I'll Sing a Song*

Johnson, Laura: *Simplified Rhythm Stick Activities*

Palmer, Hap: *Animal Antics, Easy Does It, Learning Basic Skills Through Music Volume I, Movin', Sea Gulls, Homemade Band*

Raffi: *Everything Grows, One Light, One Sun, Raffi in Concert, Rise and Shine*

Scruggs, Joe: *Deep in the Jungle*

Sharon, Lois, and Bram: *One Elephant, Mainly Mother Goose*

Stewart, Georgiana: *Bean Bag Activities and Coordination Skills, Get a Good Start, Good Morning Exercises for Kids, Preschool Aerobic Fun*

Zeitlin, Patty: *Won't You Be My Friend?*

Books

Barclay, Mary Kay, ed. *Eddie Bear's Teacher Made Folder Games—Book II.* Chanute, KS: Noah's Ark, 1987.

Beall, Pamela Conn, and Susan Hagen Nipp. *Wee Sing and Play.* Los Angeles: Price Stern Sloan Publishers, 1981.

——. *Wee Sing—Children's Songs and Finger Plays.* Los Angeles: Price Stern Sloan Publishers, 1979.

——. *Wee Sing Nursery Rhymes and Lullabies.* Los Angeles: Price Stern Sloan Publishers, 1986.

Bond, Carol Taylor. *Fee Fie Fo Fun.* Livonia, MI: Partner Press, 1989.

Bornstein, Harry, Karen Saulnier, and Lillian Hamilton, eds. *The Comprehensive Signed English Dictionary.* Washington, DC: Gallaudet University Press, 1983.

Capon, Jack. *Ball, Rope, Hoop Activities.* Belmont, CA: David Lake Publishers, 1975.

Cromwell, Liz, Dixie Hibner, and John R. Faitel. *Finger Frolics.* Livonia, MI: Partner Press, 1983.

Dowell, Ruth I. *Move Over Mother Goose.* Mt. Rainier, MD: Gryphon House, 1987.

Eisenhart, Connie, and Ruth Bell. *Pocketful of Miracles—Holiday File Folder Games, Patterns and Directions.* Livonia, MI: Partner Press, 1985.

Finch, Karen. *File Folder Games.* Greensboro, NC: Carson-Dellosa Publishing Co., 1990.

Flint Public Library, ed. *Ring O' Ring O' Roses.* Flint, MI: Flint Board of Education, 1977.

Frank, Marjorie. *I Can Make a Rainbow.* Nashville, TN: Incentive Publications, 1976.

Gilbert, La Britta. *I Can Do It! I Can Do It!* Mt. Rainier, MD: Gryphon House, 1984.

Glazer, Tom. *Do Your Ears Hang Low.* Garden City, NY: Doubleday and Co., 1980.

——. *Eye Winker, Tom Tinker, Chin Chopper.* Garden City, NY: Doubleday and Co., 1973.

Kohl, Mary Ann. *Mudworks.* Bellingham, WA: Bright Ring Publishing, 1989.

Linderman, Emma. *Teachables from Trashables.* St. Paul, MN: Redleaf Press, 1979.

Poulsson, Emilie. *Finger Plays for Nursery and Kindergarten.* New York, NY: Dover Publications, 1971.

Redleaf, Rhoda. *Teachables II.* St. Paul, MN: Redleaf Press, 1987.

Riekehof, Lottie. *The Joy of Signing.* Springfield, MO: Gospel Publishing House, 1978.

Roberts, Lynda. *Mitt Magic.* Mt. Rainier, MD: Gryphon House, 1985.

Walters, Connie, and Diane Totten. *Sing a Song All Year Long.* Minneapolis, MN: T. S. Denison and Co., 1991.

Warren, Jean, ed. *Piggyback Songs.* Everett, WA: Warren Publishing House, 1983.

——. *More Piggyback Songs.* Everett, WA: Warren Publishing House, 1984.

Warren, Jean, and Susan Shroyer. *Piggyback Songs to Sign.* Everett, WA: Warren Publishing House, 1992.

Weisman, Miss Jackie. *My Toes Are Starting to Wiggle!* Overland Park, KS: Miss Jackie Music Company, 1989.

Wilmes, Liz and Dick. *Feltboard Fun.* Dundee, IL: Building Blocks Publications, 1984.

Patterns and Directions

Rhythm Sticks

Rhythm sticks are simple to make and durable. Express your creativity in both making and using them. Cut enough dowels so each child has a set of two rhythm sticks. Make some for yourself so you can model for the children.

You will need:

* dowel sticks 3/8″ or 1/2″ in diameter (they usually come in 36″ lengths)
* sandpaper
* permanent markers
* ruler

1. Cut the dowel stick into four 9″ lengths.
2. Sand the edges and any rough spots on the length of the stick.
3. Decorate with permanent markers or have the children decorate them.
4. Optional: Seal the marker in the wood by spraying a clear sealant (shellac or enamel) on the stick. Let dry before using.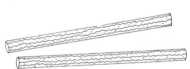

Streamers

Float, glide, and twirl in the breeze with streamers. The first variation is the easiest version to make. The second and third variations are more practical because they last longer than crepe paper streamers. Regardless of which version you choose, make one for everyone in your class, center, or group.

Variation 1

You will need:

* one or more rolls of crepe paper streamers
* optional: tape or staples and stapler
* ruler

1. Cut 12″ strips from the crepe paper roll. Give each child one streamer or multiple strips.
2. Optional: Staple or tape multiple strips together.

Variation 2

You will need:

* small waste basket size, plastic garbage bags (a variety of colors—some are even scented), or surveyors tape (plastic strips), or acquire red warning flags (from a lumber yard)
* tape or staples and stapler
* ruler

1. Cut the plastic garbage bags or red warning flags in strips about 12″ long and 1″ wide. If you are using surveyors tape, cut it in about 12″ lengths.
2. Staple or tape multiple strips together. Place a variety of colors or materials together.

Variation 3

Sheer scarves are another interesting material to use as streamers. They move differently than the crepe paper or plastic. They seem to float and work nicely with soft, slow music.

Variation 4

Taking any of the streamer materials listed above, give them a handle for this version.

You will need:

* streamer materials (any of the above)
* 3/8" dowel sticks (usually 36" lengths) or drinking straws (non-bendable ones are preferred)
* tape or staples and stapler
* ruler

1. Cut your streamers (four to six streamers per stick or straw will make it more attractive looking). Make a rainbow of colors.
2. Cut your dowel sticks into 6" or 9" lengths.
3. Holding the streamers onto one end of the dowel, tape around the stick adhering all strips firmly

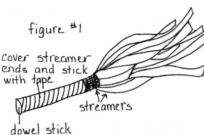

figure #1

cover streamer ends and stick with tape

streamers

dowel stick

to the stick. It is optional to tape down the whole length of the stick. Duct or electrician's tape works best. Add brightness by using colored tape.

4. If you are using a drinking straw, wrap the strips of streamers around one end of the straw and staple them to the straw. A couple of staples crisscrossed and then taped over, will hold them more firmly to the straw.

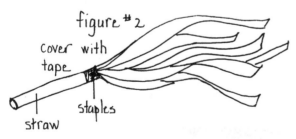

figure #2

cover with tape

straw

staples

Easel

This easel will hold boards and other items such as poster board posters, cards, or large visual aids.

You will need:

* a piece of plywood about 2' x 2' and 1/2" thick or very heavy cardboard (three-ply)

* two hinges
* nails
* saw and sander or sandpaper
* ruler
* optional: spray enamel

1. With a saw, cut out two of the easel shapes using the dimensions below.
2. Sand the edges to smooth any sharp areas.
3. Optional: Spray all sides and edges with enamel. Let dry.

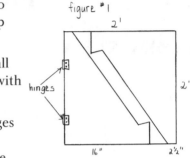

figure #1

2'

hinges

2'

16"

2½"

4. Nail the two hinges to the 2' backs about 5" from the top and the bottom. The easel folds for ease in storing.

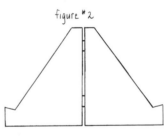

figure #2

Wands

We refer to many different types of wands throughout this book. Below are directions for making versatile wands. We have also included directions for several specific-use wands, such as star or heart wands. If you are making a wand, choose a general pattern, such as a star or heart, so it is versatile.

Basic Wand

You will need:

* fabric (felt or looped fabric are preferred because the edges do not fray)
* sewing machine, thread
* polyester filling
* stick: dowel sticks (about 12" long and 3/8" diameter), balloon sticks, straws (non-bendable), chop sticks, etc.

* saw or small knife
* sandpaper or sander
* craft glue
* scissors
* pen or pencil
* ruler
* Styrofoam ball 1″ diameter
* optional: two to three yards of satin ribbon (1/8″ or 1/4″ wide) tinsel, lace, cording, etc.

1. Draw a pattern on a double layer of fabric. Leave room to account for a seam. Cut out the pattern.

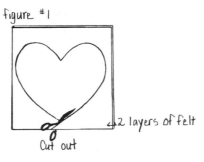

figure #1

2 layers of felt
Cut out

2. Sew around almost all of the fabric shape leaving a small opening at the bottom.

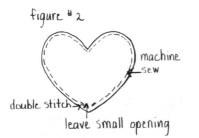

figure #2

machine sew

double stitch

leave small opening

3. If you are making your wand from fabric that frays, put the right sides of the fabric together and sew on the machine. Turn right side out and continue with the directions.

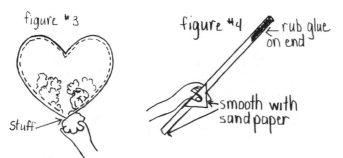

figure #3

Stuff

figure #4

rub glue on end

smooth with sandpaper

4. To reinforce the opening, double stitch at the beginning and end of the seam.

5. Fill with stuffing, leaving a small opening at the center for the stick.

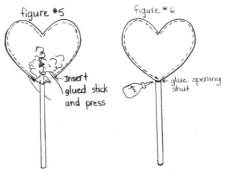

figure #5

Insert glued stick and press

figure #6

glue opening shut

6. Cut 12″ off of the dowel stick. Sand rough edges with sander or piece of sandpaper. Rub craft glue on about two inches of one end.

7. Insert the glued end into the felt object and press together so the stuffing sticks to the glue.

8. Glue the opening shut around the stick.

9. Optional: Tie a ribbon, bow, or tinsel around the stick, up near the fabric to hide the glue and add eye-appeal for the children.

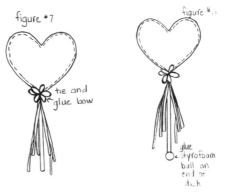

figure #7

tie and glue bow

figure #8

glue styrofoam ball on end of stick

10. If children are going to use the wand, glue a Styrofoam ball to the end of the stick for safety.

Felt Star Wand

Make a star wand out of yellow felt, using the directions for a basic wand. Decorate with glitter fabric paint to add eye-appeal. Tie and/or glue tinsel around the stick to give a twinkling effect.

figure #9

Felt Heart Wand

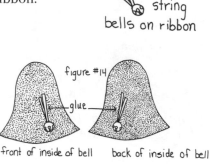

figure #10

Use the basic wand directions to create a heart wand. Before you sew a seam around the heart, insert lace between the two layers all around the edge of it. Sew the heart and lace at the same time. Tie a bow of several strands of satin ribbon around the stick. Use colors of ribbon that match the colors of the heart and lace.

Felt Fall Leaf Wand

figure #11

Orange felt makes a nice fall leaf. Use a maple leaf stencil and follow the basic wand directions to complete it. Tie strands of fall colored satin ribbon around the dowel stick and stem of the leaf.

Felt Bell Wand with Jingle Bells

This wand is different enough from the basic wand that we have added a few more directions. This wand is both visually and auditorily appealing.

You will need:

* two different colors of felt
* small jingle bells
* 12" of 1/8" wide satin ribbon
* ruler

1. Cut four bell shapes out of felt—two each of two different colors. One color will represent the inside of the bell and the other the outside. The outside color will have a curved upward bottom and the inside color will have a curved downward bottom.

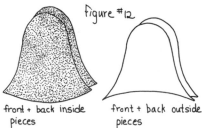

figure #12

front + back inside pieces

front + back outside pieces

2. Cut the 12" length of ribbon in half. String two small jingle bells on about 6" strands of ribbon.

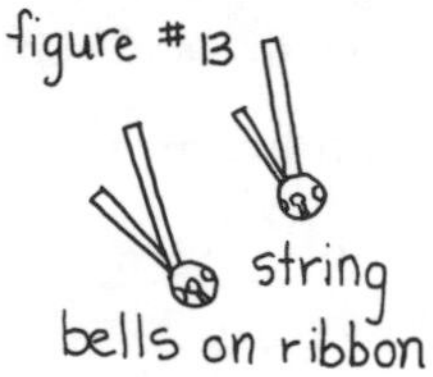

figure #13

string bells on ribbon

3. Glue the ends of the ribbons to the inside layer of the bell so it will dangle below the outside layer of the bell.

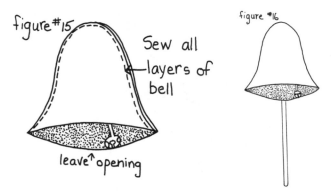

figure #14

glue

front of inside of bell

back of inside of bell

4. Sew around the outer edge of all four layers, leaving a small opening for the stick.

figure #15

Sew all layers of bell

leave opening

figure #16

5. Follow the rest of the basic wand directions (starting on step number 4) to complete the bell wand.

Looped Fabric Circle or Smiley Face Wand

Use the basic wand directions to make looped fabric wands. A circle about 5" in diameter is a good size. The versatility comes in when you are able to change the pieces on the wand.

figure #17

For a smiley face wand, use yellow looped fabric. Cut two eyes and a smile out of black stiff pellon or black poster board. Stick a small strip of hooked fastener on the back of the eyes and mouth. If the adhesive doesn't stick to the stiff pellon, apply a drop of quick bonding glue. Position facial features on the yellow circle wand.

Looped Fabric Shapes

The four basic shapes are a good start for looped fabric wands. Follow the basic wand directions. Choose your own colors. Make them all the same or different. If you use looped fabric, the possibilities for your square, triangle, rectangle, and circle will multiply.

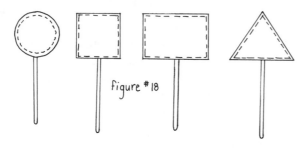

figure #18

Looped Fabric Stop and Go Wand

Using the basic wand directions, cut a red and a green circle about 6" in diameter out of looped fabric. Sew them together so red is on one side and green is on the other. Cut small stencil letters, "STOP" and "GO," out of black foam rubber place mats or poster board. Apply strips of hooked fastener to the backs and put on the wand.

figure #19

front red

back green

Styrofoam Ball Spider Wand

This is not a sewn wand. Follow the directions below to create this cute spider.

You will need:

* Styrofoam ball 3" diameter (use smaller for the little spider and larger for the big spider)
* black spray enamel
* small pom-pom for the nose (1/2" diameter)
* white fabric paint, paint brush
* eight black pipe cleaners for legs
* felt scraps for feet
* balloon stick 10" long
* scissors

* craft glue
* ruler

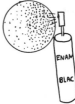

figure #20

1. Spray the Styrofoam ball and balloon stick with black enamel and let dry.

2. Glue nose on front, upper section of Styrofoam ball. Draw eyes and mouth on with white fabric paint.

3. Dip ends of eight pipe cleaners in craft glue and poke into middle section of Styrofoam ball for legs. Bend so they look like spider legs.

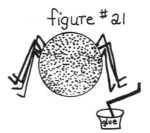

figure #21

glue

figure #22

figure #23

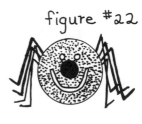

4. Cut sixteen small feet out of felt. Glue two together on the end of each pipe cleaner leg.

5. Poke the balloon stick into the bottom of the spider to use as a handle.

Waving Hand Wand

Here is a very simple and quickly made wand.

You will need:

* pop-up sponge product that swells when put in water (found at craft stores)
* balloon stick
* pen or pencil
* scissors
* craft glue

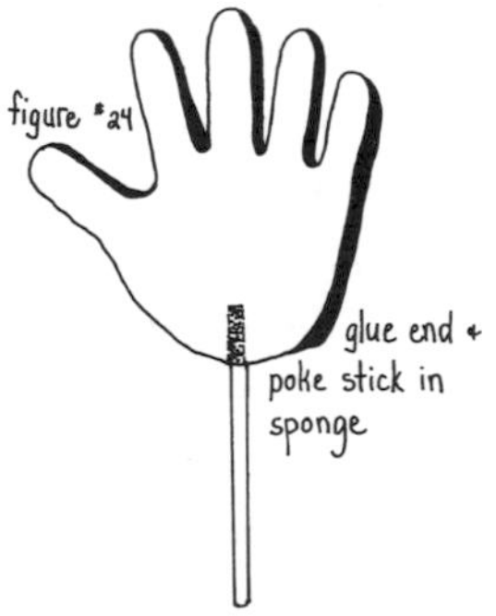

1. Trace and cut a hand shape from the pop-up sponge product.

2. Place in water so it swells to normal sponge width.

3. Dip balloon stick in craft glue and poke into bottom of sponge hand.

figure #24

glue end & poke stick in sponge

Garland Wand

Make a simple and quick wand with garland and straws.

You will need:

* ★ Christmas garland (white, silver, or gold)
* ★ straight (not flexible) straws or 3/8″ dowel sticks
* ★ staples and stapler or hot glue gun
* ★ ruler

1. Cut 5″ lengths of garland.

2. Wrap the garland around one end of the straw and staple. Or place a little hot glue on one end and wrap the garland. Hot glue guns work best with dowel sticks.

Folding Wand

Create this unusual portable wand and take your magic anywhere.

You will need:

* ★ **Three 12″ strips of 1/2″ wooden slats or a folding yard stick**
* ★ **two rivets or two tiny screws and nuts (not needed if using the folding yard stick)**
* ★ **non-toxic paints, paint brush**
* ★ **glitter glue**

1. Paint the wooden slats or folding yard stick. Use any color. Dry thoroughly.

2. Join the wooden slats with the rivets or screw and nuts in accordion fashion. (This step is omitted if you use a folding yard stick.)

3. Decorate the end of the last wooden slat (wand tip) with glitter glue.

Pointing Finger Wand

Create this variation of the basic wand.

You will need:

* ★ **12″ dowel stick**

* ★ sandpaper or sander
* ★ polyester filling
* ★ woman's dress glove
* ★ craft glue or hot glue gun
* ★ needle and thread

1. Sand the dowel and round the ends.

2. Stuff the glove with polyester filling. Place the index finger in a pointed position, the thumb and other fingers bent in and touching across the palm. Glue fingers in this position with the glue or hot glue gun. Sew or glue wrist edges together, leaving a nickel size hole in the center of the edge.

3. Attach the stuffed glove to the dowel using the hole on the edge of the wrist portion. Glue in place making sure the hand is securely attached to the dowel.

Blue Jean Circles

There are many options for sitting spaces for children. Blue jean circles are one of the most durable and practical. Wash them in the washing machine and dry in dryer. Make enough circles so each of the children in your group has their own.

You will need:

* ★ **denim fabric about one-half yard per circle**
* ★ **sewing machine, needle and heavy-duty thread**
* ★ **Styrofoam pellets**
* ★ **funnel**
* ★ **measuring cup (one cup)**
* ★ **yarn**
* ★ **scissors**
* ★ **pen or pencil**
* ★ **ruler**

1. Measure and cut two circles about 18″ in diameter from the denim fabric.

2. Place right sides together and sew 1/2″ seam almost all the way around.

3. Clip seams to allow give in fabric.

4. Turn right side out. Using a funnel, fill with a small amount (one to two cups) of Styrofoam pellets.

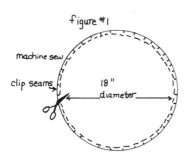

figure #1

machine sew

clip seams

18" diameter

figure #2

figure #3   sew opening shut

Thread needle with yarn

5. Hand sew opening shut with heavy-duty thread.

6. Thread needle with yarn and stitch one strand through the middle of the circle. Tie off with knot and cut yarn.

Bearskin Rug

Create this soft and inviting rug for group seating.

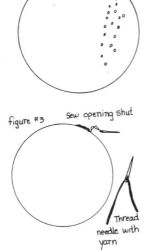

Cut double head— sew together & stuff for 3-D effect.

You will need:

* 3 yards of 60" wide artificial fur material (This size material seats six to eight children. Vary the size according to the number of children you wish to accommodate.)

* polyester filling

* scissors

* sewing machine, needle and thread

* scraps of fabric for the eyes, ears, nose, and mouth

1. Cut a bear shape out of the material as illustrated. Be sure to make the legs wide enough for a child to sit on. Because the fur material does not unravel, it is not necessary to stitch the cut edges.

2. Cut a second head shape with scrap pieces.

3. Sew the two head pieces together (right sides facing one another) and turn the head right side out. Stuff the head with polyester filling and close the opening with a basting stitch.

4. Decorate the head as your sewing skills and creativity allow. Add ears, eyes, nose, and mouth from scraps of material, buttons, felt, etc.

Pillows

Pillows are soft and pleasant to cuddle. Here are two different variations of pillows—the first one children make and use; with the second variation, you make and children use.

Small Pillows

This activity is fun and creative. Children can design their own pillow. Follow the directions below to make a versatile item that is used throughout the year. As children leave your program, they can take this special and meaningful item with them.

You will need:

* a white or light-colored solid flat bed sheet

* permanent markers or fabric paints

* polyester stuffing

* sewing machine, needle and thread

* scissors

* ruler

* newspaper or vinyl tablecloth

* tape

1. Cut your sheet into pieces about 10" square.

2. Lay newspaper or a vinyl tablecloth on the table where children will be working.

3. Give each child one piece of cloth and let them create a design or draw a picture of themselves with permanent markers or fabric paint. Make sure to get a variety of colors, especially for different colored skin, hair, and eyes. Because this fabric is flimsy, tape the corners down so it is easier for the children to draw on.

4. After the design has dried (especially if they used fabric paint), place their designed fabric on top of another piece of fabric. With both layers, cut subtle curves

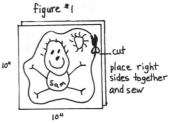

figure #1

10"

10"

cut

place right sides together and sew

Sam

all around the design. You could leave it a square too, but cutting a shape makes it more unique.

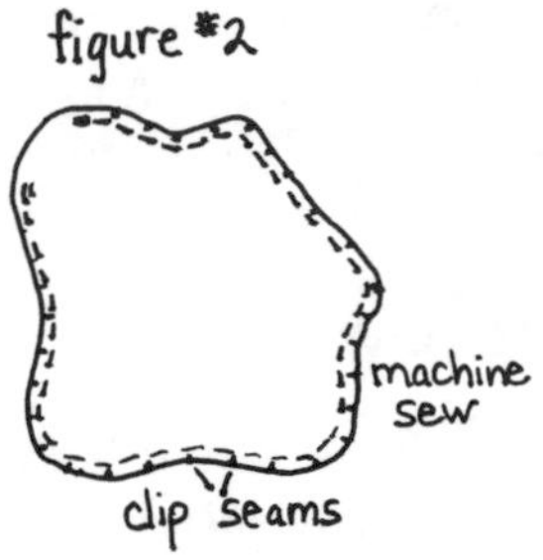

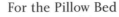
figure #2

5. Turn the pieces so the right sides are together and machine sew all around the edge leaving about a 3" opening.

machine sew

clip seams

6. Clip seams so fabric gives and turn right side out.

figure #3

stuffing

stuff and then sew opening shut.

Sam

7. Children can now fill their pillow with polyester stuffing.

8. Hand sew the opening shut and you are done.

Pillow Babies and Beds

Pillow babies are an abstract looking baby in a pillow bed made of matching fabric. Children can learn nurturing skills with this soft to the touch item. Make several pillow babies, one for each child in your group.

You will need:

* scrap pieces of various colors and textures of fabric (knit, satin, corduroy, fur, etc.). You may have scraps of fabric around the house or fabric stores may give you miscellaneous pieces. It is nice to get at least the primary and secondary colors or different skin colors.

* polyester stuffing

* optional: purchased eyes or buttons, floss and/or fabric paint

* sewing machine, needle and thread

* scissors

* ruler

1. For each bed and baby, double your fabric to cut two layers of the following: an oval (7" long and 5" wide) and a rectangle (9" x 7"). Then cut a single square (7" x 7"). All of these should be cut out of the same fabric.

For the Pillow Bed

2. Sew a small hem on one side of the 7" x 7" square.

3. Taking the rectangles, place them so right sides are together with the square in between them. Sew most of the way around these pieces, leaving a 2" opening for stuffing. Clip corners.

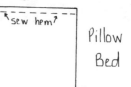
figure #1

sew hem

Pillow Bed

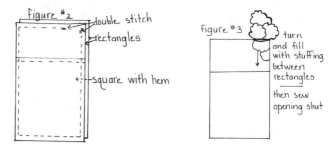
figure #2
double stitch
rectangles
square with hem

figure #3
turn and fill with stuffing between rectangles
then sew opening shut

4. Turn them right sides out and put a small amount of polyester stuffing in the rectangle shape.

5. Hand sew the opening shut. Now you have a pillow bed with a cover to tuck your baby in.

For the Pillow Baby

2. If you want a face on your baby, take one oval and sew eyes on the upper section of the oval. Put a nose and mouth on using floss or fabric paint. Note: A face is not necessary—children are good at using their imagination.

figure #4
optional-button eyes and embroidered nose and mouth

3. Taking the oval shapes, place them right sides together and sew a 1/4" seam all around the edge, leaving a 2" opening.

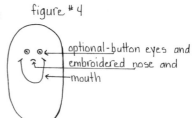
figure #5
double stitch
clip seams

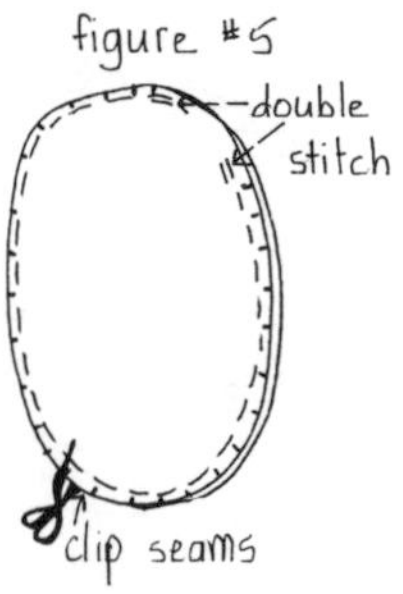

figure #6
Turn, stuff and sew opening shut

4. Clip seams so fabric gives and turn right side out. Stuff a little, and hand sew the opening shut.

Decorative Felt Bags

Use these cute little bags for many magical activities. Be creative in designing, decorating, and using small felt bags.

You will need:

* ★ felt squares
* ★ patterns for bags
* ★ sewing machine, needle and thread
* ★ 6″ lengths of 1/4″ satin ribbon
* ★ miscellaneous materials to decorate bags
* ★ electronic music buttons (found in most craft stores)
* ★ scissors
* ★ pen or pencil
* ★ glue or hot glue gun
* ★ ruler

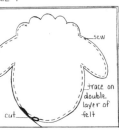

figure #1

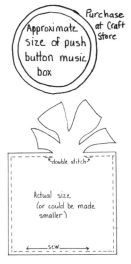

1. Choose a pattern for your bag. Some choices are provided or create your own. Put two pieces of felt back to back and trace the pattern on them.

2. Machine sew about 1/4″ in from traced outline. Stitch around most of the pattern, leaving an opening to insert your music button or any other small item you desire. To reinforce the opening, double stitch at the beginning and end of the seam.

3. Cut out on traced line.

4. If you want a handle, cut out a 6″ length of 1/4″ wide ribbon. Attach with needle and thread onto both sides of the bag.

figure #2

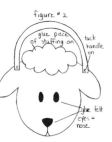

5. Glue decorations on your bag for added appeal (a leaf on the apple, a bow on the package, and so on).

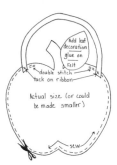

Music Booklet and Easel

A music booklet comes in handy for various times during the day. Keep the words, illustrations, and chords for children's favorite songs on hand for those times when you need some music to help a transition.

You will need:

* ★ large sheet of poster board
* ★ colored contact paper
* ★ scissors
* ★ paper punch
* ★ 5″ x 8″ index cards
* ★ two 1″ metal book rings
* ★ ruler
* ★ optional: permanent markers and decorations, such as vinyl letters and stickers

For Booklet Front and Back Covers

1. Cut two booklet covers (front and back) about 5 1/2″ x 8 1/2″ each out of poster board.

2. Cover them with colored contact paper and decorate creatively with permanent markers, vinyl letters, or stickers.

For Booklet Easel

3. Cut two easel patterns out of the poster board.

4. Lay the two pieces, backs together, about 1/4″ apart on colored contact paper. Cover the top with another piece of colored contact paper and cut out, leaving the two pieces connected by the seam between the two backs.

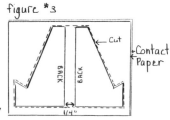

figure #2 - Easel

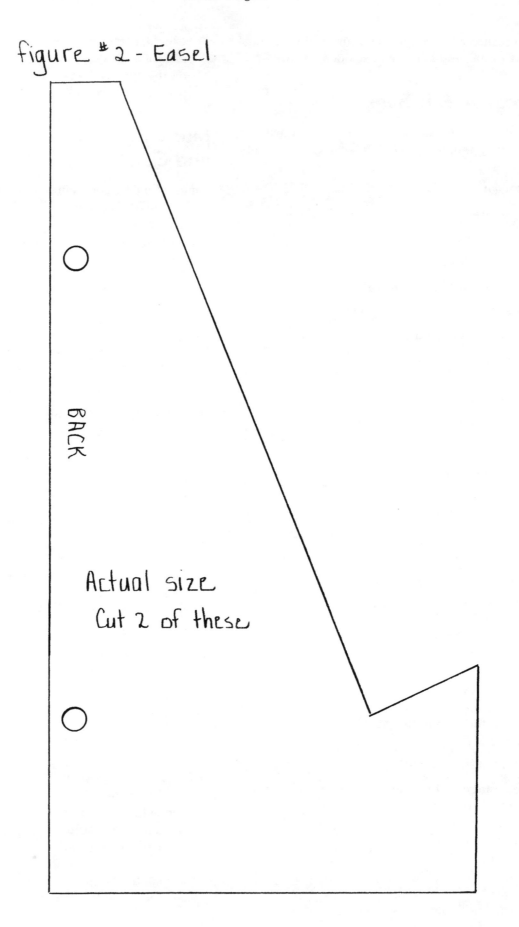

BACK

Actual size
Cut 2 of these

figure #2 - Easel

5. Write words, chords, and illustrations of songs on the index cards.

6. Punch two holes in the index cards, cover, and easel. Hook together with metal book rings.

Now you have your booklet with favorite songs, chords, illustrations, and easel all together. As you learn more songs, add more index cards to your music booklet.

Beanbags

Basic Beanbag

Make beanbags out of various materials. If you are going to use the beanbags for many activities throughout the year, use a durable fabric like denim. Consider cutting your pieces from discarded blue jean pants or skirt.

You will need:

* fabric (denim, polyester knit, cotton)

* filler, such as Styrofoam pellets, popcorn seeds, navy beans, or rice

* sewing machine, needle and heavy-duty thread

* funnel

* pen or pencil

* ruler

figure #1

double stitch

sew →

clip seam corners

1. Choose a basic shape for your beanbag, such as a circle or square. Trace the shape onto your fabric and cut it either 5″ in diameter or 5″ long.

2. On the sewing machine, with right sides together, stitch a 1/4″ seam. Sew around the whole shape leaving only about a 1″ opening. To reinforce the opening, double stitch at the beginning and end of sewing.

3. Clip notches around the seam of the circle or cut off the corners of the square. Turn the bag right side out.

4. Pour filler into the bag using a funnel until the bag is about three-fourths full. If you use popcorn, navy beans, or rice, make sure your beanbags do not get soaking wet or the seeds will swell and the bag will be ruined.

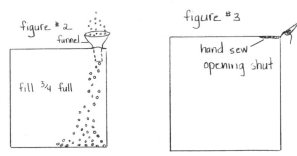

figure #2
funnel
fill ¾ full

figure #3
hand sew opening shut

5. Hand stitch the opening shut with heavy duty thread.

Felt Shape Beanbags

It is nice to have some beanbags of various shapes and colors that go with different themes to enhance learning. If you do a unit on fruits, make various felt fruit beanbags such as an apple, orange, pear, watermelon slice, and strawberry. Plan to do many activities throughout the fruit discussion with them. The advantages of felt are that it comes in so many colors and the raw edges don't fray so you do not need to turn them inside out when sewing. Because felt is not as durable as a fabric such as denim, however, put them away when the unit is complete.

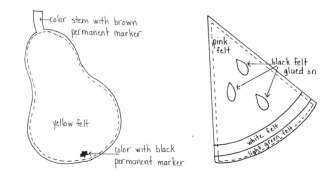

color stem with brown permanent marker
yellow felt
color with black permanent marker
pink felt
black felt glued on
white felt
light green felt

You will need:

* felt in various colors

* poster board stencils or cookie cutters of desired shapes

* permanent markers or fabric paints

* sewing machine, needle and heavy-duty thread

* filler, such as Styrofoam pellets, popcorn seeds, navy beans, or rice

* scraps of felt or fabric for decorations

* glue or hot glue gun

* scissors

★ funnel

★ pen or pencil

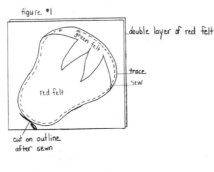

figure #1

double layer of red felt

green felt

trace
sew

red felt

cut on outline
after sewn

1. Use poster board stencils or cookie cutters to trace the desired shapes on a piece of felt.

2. Place two pieces together. If you are using other colors (additional layers) of felt to enhance the design, such as in the leaves on the strawberry, cut and place those pieces on before sewing. Machine sew through all layers, about 1/4" in from the traced outline. Sew almost all the way around the shape. To reinforce the opening, double stitch at the beginning and end of sewing.

3. Cut along the traced outline.

4. Using the funnel, pour filler into the beanbag until it is about three-fourths full.

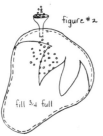

figure #2

fill 3/4 full

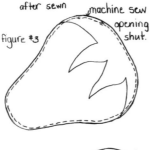

after sewn

machine sew
opening
shut.

figure #3

5. With the needle and thread, sew the opening shut.

6. Add decorative features with permanent markers, fabric paint, and/or glued-on felt scraps.

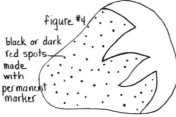

figure #4

black or dark red spots made with permanent marker

Sock Bean Bags

You can make nice bean bags by simply pouring and tying.

You will need:

★ baby socks (nylon or tube)

★ yarn

★ filler, such as Styrofoam pellets, popcorn seeds, navy beans, or rice

1. Pour the filler into half of the sock foot.

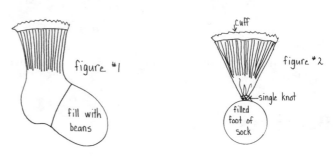

figure #1

fill with beans

cuff

figure #2

single knot

filled foot of sock

2. Tie the sock into a single knot by the heel.

3. Turn the cuff of the sock down so it surrounds the part with the pellets (this gives the beanbag double durability).

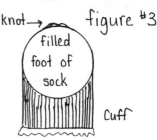

knot→

figure #3

filled foot of sock

cuff

4. Gather the top of the cuff together. Using a small strand of yarn, tie a double knot around the gathered section.

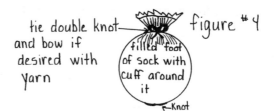

tie double knot and bow if desired with yarn

figure #4

filled foot of sock with cuff around it

Knot

Pom-Poms

Although there are pom-pom makers, making your own allows you to choose colors, sizes, and thickness. They take about ten to fifteen minutes to make and provide children with hours of delight.

Variation 1

You will need:

★ four-ply or rug yarn

★ scissors

★ optional: 3" to 4" square of thick cardboard

1. Wrap the yarn around the palm of your hand or cut a square piece of cardboard the desired size of your pom-poms (about 3" to 4") and wrap the

yarn around that. Continue wrapping until you have the desired thickness (about one-third of a typical skein per pom-pom).

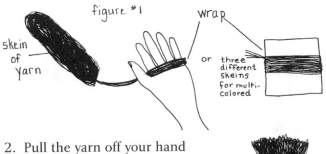

figure #1

skein of yarn

wrap

or three different skeins for multi-colored

2. Pull the yarn off your hand or cardboard, squeezing the center of the loops together.

figure #2

3. Tightly tie another piece of yarn around the center of the loops. Tie a knot on one side, turn your pom-pom over and tie another knot on the other side, for security.

4. Cut all of the loops and shake the pom-pom out.

figure #3

loops

tie knots on both sides of loops

figure #4

cut all loop ends

5. Trim any ragged edges and the yarn that you tied around the center of the loops, forming an evenly rounded ball shape.

figure #5

trim ragged edges

Make several pom-poms. Create multi-colored ones by mixing colors of yarn together. Pull one strand of two or three colors of yarn and wrap them around your hand or cardboard at the same time. This also speeds up the wrapping process.

Variation 2

If you don't want to be bothered with all of the wrapping, try this variation of the pom-pom. Use rug yarn, which is folded perfectly for this variation.

You will need:

* **rug yarn**
* **scissors**

1. Unfold your skein of rug yarn as far as you can so it is laid out in long loops. Then cut one end of the loops. Lay out yarn in long lengths.

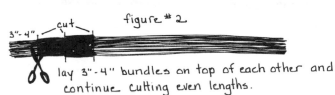

figure #1

skein of rug yarn

unwrap skein & cut 1 end

yarn laid out in long length.

2. Choose a length for your pom pom and cut that much yarn (usually 3" to 4" long). Place that bundle of yarn on top of the end of the yarn lengths and continue cutting until you have as much yarn in your bundle as you want it thick (usually one-third of the skein).

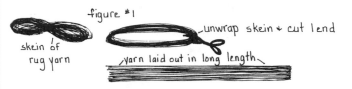

3"-4"   cut   figure #2

lay 3"-4" bundles on top of each other and continue cutting even lengths.

3. Now gather your large bundle of yarn in your hand, squeezing it together in the middle. Take a separate piece of yarn and tie it tightly around the center of the bundle. Double tying will make it more secure.

figure #3

squeeze together. then tie double knot

4. Shake your bundle out and trim the ragged edges so it is in the form of a nicely rounded ball.

figure #4

cut ragged edges

5. Make multi-colored pom-poms with this variation, also. Lay out two or three skeins of different colored yarn and cut your bundles, laying them on top of each other.

figure #5

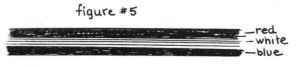

—red
—white
—blue

Riddle Box

You will need:

* a small box about 12″ square
* pictures related to a special theme or new vocabulary words
* colored contact paper
* sheets of paper
* pen or pencil
* scissors

1. Cover the box with colored contact paper or construction paper.

2. Choose pictures for four to six sides of the box. On each side of the box, tape a picture.

3. Make up a riddle that describes each picture.

4. Write each riddle on a sheet of paper large enough to cover the picture.

5. Cover the picture with the appropriate riddle. Tape the riddle in such a way that you can lift up the paper after the children have correctly guessed the riddle.

6. Change these pictures and riddles and bring out your riddle box again to grab the children's attention.

Finger Play Book

You will need:

* 5″ x 8″ index cards
* index tabs

* paper punch
* two 2″ metal book rings
* poster board
* markers
* contact paper
* optional: choose other materials to make a durable, attractive cover

1. Collect your favorite finger plays. Tape or print the words and actions on 5″ x 8″ cards, one per side.

2. Categorize finger plays by season, holiday, or thematic unit. List categories in a table of contents.

3. Make a divider card for each category and attach an index tab. Stagger tabs for an easy location.

4. For the cover, cut a piece of poster board the size of the index cards. Use your creativity to decorate the cover and make your book bright and attractive.

5. If you use paper, cover with contact paper.

6. Punch two holes in each index card and the cover. A side opening is preferable for laying in your lap, but a top opening works, too.

7. Optional: Attach a garland wand (page 90) to your finger play book. Poke a hole through the end of the straw and slip it on the metal book ring that holds your finger play book together.

Stretchies

Stretchies are simple to make and easy to store. Children are interested in using stretchies to make their bodies move in many different ways. Follow the directions below to make stretchies for each child in your group.

You will need:

* a 6′ length of 1/2″ elastic for each child
* scissors
* sewing machine
* ruler
* optional: permanent markers

1. Cut your elastic into 6′ lengths. Shorter lengths snap when stretching and can smart on the children's skin.

2. Machine sew the ends together so you finish with a circle. Make sure you sew back and forth a few times so it is secure.

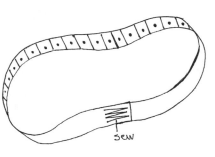

3. Optional: Decorate a design on the elastic with permanent markers. Older children may be able to do this.

Now have fun. Watch the children's creative abilities and critical thinking develop.

Pocket Aprons

Aprons serve many purposes. Wear one to cover up your clothes during a messy activity. Store items in a pocket apron. Use a felt or looped fabric apron as an activity board. Below are two variations for making aprons. Combine characteristics of each to make the perfect apron for your needs.

Variation 1

This apron has a front and back side with several pockets.

You will need:

* fabric for the apron, ties, and pockets (denim, felt, looped fabric, or heavy cotton). Mix and match your fabrics on your denim apron, sew looped fabric pockets on one side and felt

pockets on the other, etc. The length of the fabric will be determined by your size and how long you want it (about 1 yard of 60″ width).

* pattern pieces made of newspaper or tissue
* buttons, snaps, hooked fastener
* sewing machine, needle and thread
* scissors
* ruler
* optional: shoelaces, ribbon, etc.

1. Cut two identical apron shapes to fit your figure. (Use newspaper or tissue for your pattern pieces.) Cut any number of pockets in varying sizes. Cut a long strip for four ties or use shoelaces, ribbon, etc.

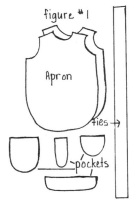

2. If you have fabric with fraying edges, take two long strips of your fabric about 1-1/2″ wide, and the length of your neck opening. Hem both sides of strip. Then fold them around your neck opening and sew them on.

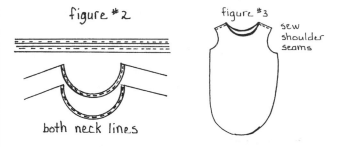

3. Machine sew the shoulder seams together with right sides facing each other.

4. If you have a fabric that has fraying edges, turn them under twice and machine sew a thin hem all around the outer edge of the apron.

5. If you are using the same fabric for the ties as you used for the apron, cut lengths 1-1/2" wide and 48" long. Fold both fraying edges in and then fold one more time in half, the long way. Sew along the 48" strip. Cut it into four 12" lengths. If you use ribbon or shoelaces for the ties, this step will not be necessary.

6. Machine sew your ties onto your apron about even with your waist and 1" overlapping the under side of your apron.

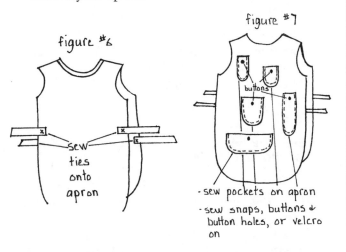

7. Sew your pockets onto the apron. Put them on one or both sides of your apron. Remember, if you have fraying edges, you will need to sew hems all around the pockets before sewing them onto your apron.

8. With the needle and thread, sew buttons and button holes, snaps, or adhere hooked fasteners onto the pockets. Now they can be closed to keep your items in.

Variation 2

This apron has a front side with one big pocket. These instructions will be for looped fabric, so it will not include all of the directions for sewing hems in the fraying edges. If you are using a fraying fabric, follow the instructions for variation 1 to hem your edges.

You will need:

* looped fabric large enough to cover the front portion of your body and make one big pocket (about 1/2 yard of 60" width)

* pattern made of newspaper or tissue

* binding tape (can be purchased at a fabric store) about 6'

* sewing machine, needle and thread

* hooked fastener about 3"

* scissors

1. Pin pattern on looped fabric and cut apron shape and pocket.

2. Cut the hooked fastener into three 1" pieces, space them evenly on the top edge of the pocket and hand sew them on so they are securely fastened.

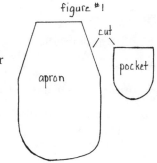

3. Machine sew the pocket onto the apron.

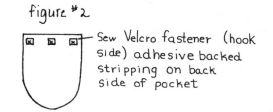

4. Cut a piece of binding tape so it fits around your neck and attaches to the top corners of your apron. Make this opening large enough to pull the apron on over your head. The ends of binding tape should overlap about 1" onto your apron.

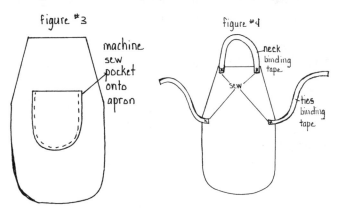

5. Machine or hand sew binding tape to the top corners of your apron (double or triple sew for security).

6. Cut the remainder of binding tape in half and machine or hand sew the strips to each side of your apron, waist high. These are the ties that will go around your back.

Now you have an apron with a pocket that can also serve as a looped fabric board.

Looped Fabric Cube

A looped fabric cube is similar to a large die. The advantage of this item is that pieces are removable. Put different symbols on to fit the concept at hand. Teach children their colors by making stiff pellon circles of different colors with a strip of hooked fastener on the back. Place the primary colors (red, yellow, and blue) and secondary colors (green, orange, and purple) on the cube. If you are working with older children, put letters of the alphabet onto your cube. There are unlimited possibilities.

You will need:

* ★ looped fabric
* ★ polyester stuffing
* ★ stencils for cutting pieces such as numerals, shapes, letters, animals
* ★ material for the pieces such as poster board, rubber place mats, stiff pellon
* ★ hooked fastener stripping
* ★ sewing machine, needle and thread
* ★ pen or pencil
* ★ scissors
* ★ ruler
* ★ optional: quick bonding glue

The materials listed are for both the looped fabric cube and the hooked fastener pieces.

For the Looped Fabric Cube

1. Cut looped fabric into six equal squares. About 8" or 9" squares are a good size.

2. Place two squares on top of each other, wrong sides together (loop side out). Machine sew a 1/3" seam along one side. You want the raw edges on the outside so when you stuff the cube it will maintain its shape. This fabric does not fray. Always double stitch the beginning and the end of the seam.

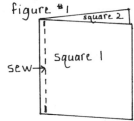

3. Taking another square, join two sides, one to each of the previous sewn squares. You now have half of the cube.

4. Continue adding squares, sewing them to form a cube. Leave one seam open.

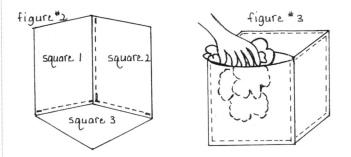

5. Stuff a small amount of polyester stuffing into the open seam. You do not need much because you do not want your cube to bulge out on the sides. If it does bulge, the cube will not land flat on one side when you roll it.

6. With needle and thread, stitch the final seam shut.

For the Hooked Fastener Pieces

7. Use the stencils to outline pieces of your choice. Use any of the materials listed above, providing they are stiff. Cut out each piece.

8. Adhere small strips of hooked fastener to the back of each piece. The heavier your pieces are, the more hooked fastener you will want to use. For example, on rubber place mats put a small strip on each edge of the piece. You need little on stiff pellon—just a small strip in the middle of your piece will do the trick.

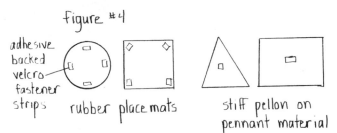

9. If the hooked fastener strips are not sticking, squeeze a small drop of quick bonding glue on the back and position on the piece.

Place your pieces on your cube and you are ready to have loads of fun with this versatile item!

Movement Mats

Foam rubber or vinyl place mats are durable materials used for many activities with children. One use of rubber place mats is for stretcher activities. Below are directions for placing stenciled symbols of different shapes on the mats.

You will need:

* ★ rubber or vinyl place mats; plain, solid colored ones are the best (look for sales—sometimes you can get seasonal ones for a low price)
* ★ solid colored or printed contact paper
* ★ stencils, such as geometric shapes, numerals, letters, animals
* ★ pen or pencil
* ★ scissors
* ★ optional: poster board

1. On the back of the colored contact paper, trace a stencil. Remember to trace the stencil backwards so when you cut it out it is positioned correctly.

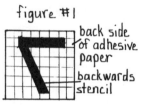

figure #1

back side of adhesive paper

backwards stencil

2. Cut out the stenciled symbols and pull the paper off the back of the contact paper.

figure #2

cut stencil

peel paper off back

3. Place the contact paper symbol on the foam rubber place mat.

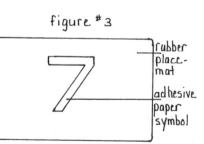

figure #3

rubber place-mat

adhesive paper symbol

If you are trying to economize, replace place mats with poster board that has been scrounged from a printing company. Cut the poster board into a desired size and shape and cover with clear or colored contact paper. Now continue from step 1 to put colored contact paper symbols on your poster board mats. Cut poster board symbols to fit the program's focus or theme. Make different bugs for an insect unit, or stars for a space theme.

Pom-Pom Pals

Pom-pom pals are soft and pleasant to the touch—and versatile. Put these pals in the last of your nesting containers. Use them as the tip of a tiny wand or hide one in the smallest of places. A small magnet or metal tack on the bottom enables the pom-pom pal to follow the curving path with the help of a magnetic wand (see page 113). Make several at a time.

You will need:

* ★ small craft pom-poms (found in most craft stores)
* ★ 1″ pom-pom for the body
* ★ 1/4″ pom-pom for the nose
* ★ 7 mm pom-poms for the eyes
* ★ small piece of stiff pellon or poster board; about 1-1/2″ square
* ★ craft glue
* ★ scissors

1. Cut the stiff pellon or poster board into feet shape.

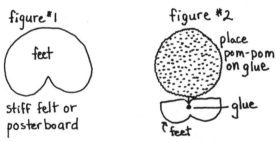

figure #1

feet

stiff felt or posterboard

figure #2

place pom-pom on glue

glue

feet

2. Drip a small amount of glue in the center of the feet and place the 1″ pom-pom on it.

3. Drip three small drops of glue on the upper section of the 1″ pom-pom in a triangular shape.

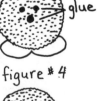

figure #3

glue

4. Place the 7mm pom-poms on the two upper drops of glue and the 1/4″ pom-pom on the lower drop.

figure #4

eyes
nose

Vary the sizes of the materials to make larger or smaller pom-pom pals.

Note: If you have children who still put objects in their mouth, choose something else for this activity or use larger pom-poms.

Song-Choosing Visual Aids

Window Shade Chart

This is a durable visual aid to use year after year. Use a shade that covers a window so it has a dual purpose. Even if you don't have shades on your windows, consider this charting option.

You will need:

* small window shade
* permanent markers

figure #1

Mary Had A Little Lamb
The Itsy Bitsy Spider
Rain Rain Go Away
The Wheels on the Bus
If You're Happy and You Know It

1. Before hanging the shade, use the permanent markers to neatly print titles of some of the children's favorite songs onto it.

2. Add pictures next to the song titles that indicate what the song is, so children also benefit from this visual aid.

3. Mount the shade on a window or wall.

If you want to give children fewer choices, pull the shade down part way. If you want them to have a large variety, pull it down the entire way.

Song Flowers

This is a simple visual aid. Make your own flower stencil or use the one provided below. Making various colored flowers is eye-appealing and gives children one more way to learn colors.

You will need:

* various colors of poster board
* flower stencil
* colored circular coding labels about 1″ in diameter (found in office supply stores)
* laminating machine
* pen or pencil
* scissors
* craft glue
* permanent markers
* vase for displaying flowers

* optional: juice can and colored contact paper

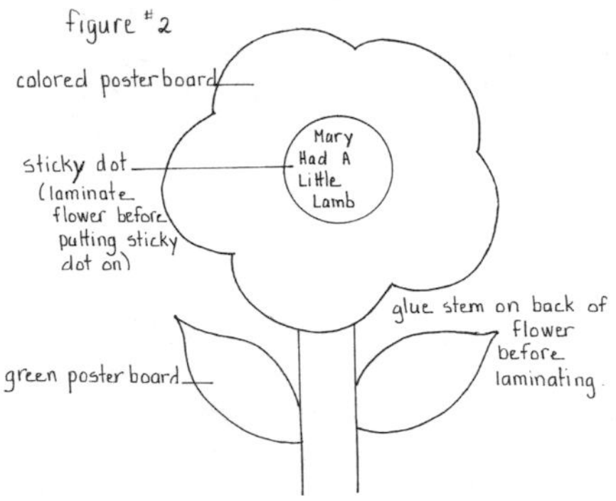

1. Trace flower and stem stencil on back of colored poster board.

2. Cut it out.

3. Glue stem to back of flower.

figure #2

colored posterboard

sticky dot (laminate flower before putting sticky dot on)

Mary Had A Little Lamb

glue stem on back of flower before laminating

green posterboard

4. Laminate the flower and stem.

5. Print favorite songs on colored circular coding labels with permanent markers and position it in the center of the flower.

6. Optional: Instead of a purchased vase, cover an empty juice can with colored contact paper.

7. Store flowers in the vase.

Deck of Songs

This visual is small and easily stored near your group area. Children will enjoy choosing songs to sing during those short wait times.

You will need:

* poster board
* water-based markers
* clear contact paper
* hand drawings, rubber stamps, or stickers that resemble the songs
* scissors
* craft glue
* ruler
* optional: colored contact paper

1. Cut several 5″ x 8″ rectangles from the poster board.

2. With the markers, print the title of a song on each card.

3. Draw, stamp, or glue a picture of the song on the card.

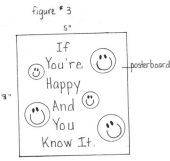

figure #3

If You're Happy And You Know It.

posterboard

Sometimes you can find stickers that resemble the songs (farm animals, food items, nursery rhymes).

4. Cover each card, both front and back, with contact paper for durability. Cover the front with clear contact paper and the back with either printed or clear contact paper.

Spinner Story Board

Use this versatile board for spinner board stories.

You will need:

* a 20″ square piece of poster board or large pizza cardboard (about 18″ in diameter)
* scrap pieces of poster board
* colored permanent markers
* 12″ adhesive looped fabric stripping
* 12″ adhesive hooked fastener stripping
* brad fastener
* ruler

1. Use the circular pizza cardboard or cut a circle with an 18″ diameter from the poster board.

2. Divide the circle into six equal wedges, using a dark permanent marker.

3. Attach a 1″ square piece of looped fabric to the center of each wedge.

4. Poke a hole in the center of the circle and attach an arrow shaped pointer made from poster board scraps. Use a brad fastener.

5. Prepare story starter shapes with scrap poster board and permanent markers. Include items such as a sun, moon, horse, cow, dog, cat, house, barn, flowers, trees, boy, girl, man, woman, apple.

6. Attach a 1″ square of hooked fastener to the center of each story starter shape.

Group Color Bingo Game

This board is used to play the group color bingo extender found on page 57.

You will need:

* one large piece of poster board about 2′ x 3′
* scrap pieces of poster board

* colored markers
* 12″ adhesive looped fabric stripping
* 12″ adhesive hooked fastener stripping
* clear contact paper (5 to 6 feet)
* scissors
* ruler

1. Divide the large piece of poster board into nine equal rectangles. Mark the lines with a dark marker.

2. Draw puddle shapes in each of the nine rectangles on the poster board. Color the shapes using these colors: red, yellow, blue, green, orange, purple, white, black, and brown.

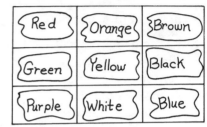

3. Cover the game board with clear contact paper.

4. Attach a 1″ square of looped fabric to the center of each color puddle.

5. Use scrap poster board and color twelve 2″ square pieces in the following colors: red, yellow, blue, green, orange, purple, white, black, brown, pink, tan, and gray. These are the calling cards for the game. Cover each with clear contact paper.

6. Attach a 1″ square hooked fastener to the center of each of the twelve calling cards.

File Folder Activities

Folder activities teach concepts such as numbers, shapes, colors, and letters. Some key factors make folder activities durable and eye-appealing to children. Follow the directions below to make a matching activity with an emphasis on numbers and an insect theme. Then, using these basic directions and tips, create your own folders. With these file folder activities, everything is stored together so children can independently get, play with, and put away the file folder.

You will need:

* file folders; colored ones are especially attractive

* shapes for matching; such as stickers, paper shapes you draw and cut out, small notepads in various shapes, rubber stamps, or colored contact paper you cut into shapes

* pocket for storing pieces; such as an envelope or sandwich size reclosable plastic bag

* clear contact paper

* craft glue

* water based markers

* loop and hook fasteners

* scissors

* X-acto knife

1. Choose a topic for your folder activity. If you are talking about insects, find small notepads that are the shape of bees, ladybugs, spiders, etc. They usually come in packets of fifty sheets. That will be plenty to make a file folder game.

2. Choose the concept for your folder game, such as numbers or colors. To reinforce the numbers one through ten, use ten sheets of your notepad. On ten of the insect shapes, write the numerals 1 through 10. On the other ten, draw dots or place colored circular coding labels (about 1/4" in diameter) on the insect shapes corresponding to the numerals 1 through 10.

figure #1 — label insects with numerals 1-10 and dots 1-10

3. Glue the entire back of each shape that has a numeral on it. As you glue them, place them at random or in sequence on the inside of your folder. Sequencing the numeral insects teaches children left to right and top to bottom progression.

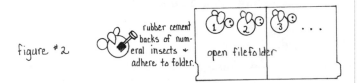

figure #2 — rubber cement backs of numeral insects & adhere to folder. open file folder

4. Cover both sides of the insect shaped pieces (with the dots) with clear contact paper. Space them a small distance apart. Cut out each piece leaving a small lip of contact paper around the edges.

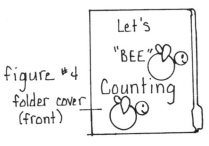

figure #3 — cover both sides with adhesive paper — adhesive paper — cut leaving small lip around edges

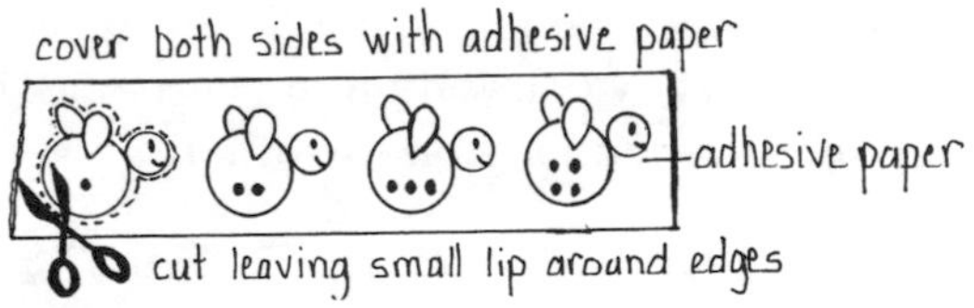

5. On the folder, label the cover with the name of the activity. Decorate by gluing two or three sheets of the notepad on it. The title and pictures will help you and the children identify the activity without opening up the folder. It also adds eye-appeal for the children.

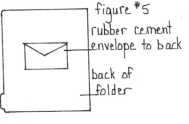

figure #4 — folder cover (front) — Let's "BEE" Counting

6. Apply glue to the entire back of your envelope and place it on the back of the folder (in the middle). This will be used to store your pieces.

figure #5 — rubber cement envelope to back — back of folder

7. Cover both the inside and outside of the folder with clear contact paper, including the envelope. Trim edges of paper.

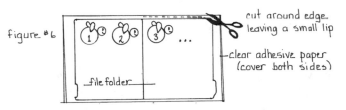

figure #6 — file folder — cut around edge leaving a small lip — clear adhesive paper (cover both sides)

8. Using the X-acto knife, carefully cut a slit through the contact paper, along the flap of the envelope. Now the outside of your envelope will be covered for durability and will also open to store your pieces.

figure #7 — cut slit along flap of envelope with x-acto knife — back of folder

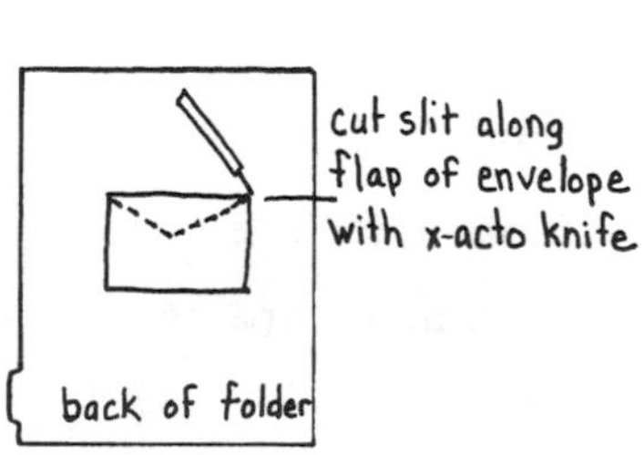

9. Put your insect shaped pieces with the dots in the envelope. Close by placing a small piece of loop

and hook fastener on the tip on the envelope flap and directly below it on the envelope (hook on one side and loop on the other).

figure #8

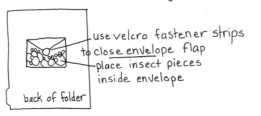

use velcro fastener strips to close envelope flap
place insect pieces inside envelope
back of folder

Tips:

* If you are using plastic file folders, which are durable, it isn't necessary to cover them with clear contact paper. Not all stickers or glued pieces stick well to this surface, however. Colored contact paper sticks the best. If the items do not stick, apply quick bonding glue to them.

* If you are using a reclosable plastic bag to store your pieces, cover the folder with clear contact paper before you put the bag on. Then tape all edges of the bag to the folder with wide clear tape. Leave the top flap where it zips shut untaped so you can open and shut it easily.

Involvement Activity Bulletin Board

Involvement activity bulletin boards are limited only by your imagination and creativity. They display matching, counting or math; critical thinking; and/or sequencing activities. Below are directions for just one type of involvement board.

You will need:

* light blue looped fabric the size of your bulletin board
* hooked fastener strips
* dark blue cording for the fish bowl border
* pins or staples and stapler
* scissors
* colored poster board
* sandpaper for the bottom of the fish bowl
* green felt for the seaweed

* laminating machine
* scissors
* craft glue or hot glue gun
* optional: looped fabric cube with numerals from 1 to 6 on it (page 101)

1. Staple or pin the light blue looped fabric over the entire bulletin board. Note: Staples are preferred if possible because they lessen the chance of children getting poked as they manipulate the board.

figure #1

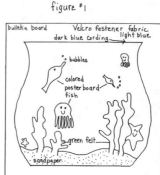

bulletin board   Velcro fastener fabric
dark blue cording   light blue
bubbles
colored poster board fish
green felt
sandpaper

2. Make fish bowl outline with dark blue cording.

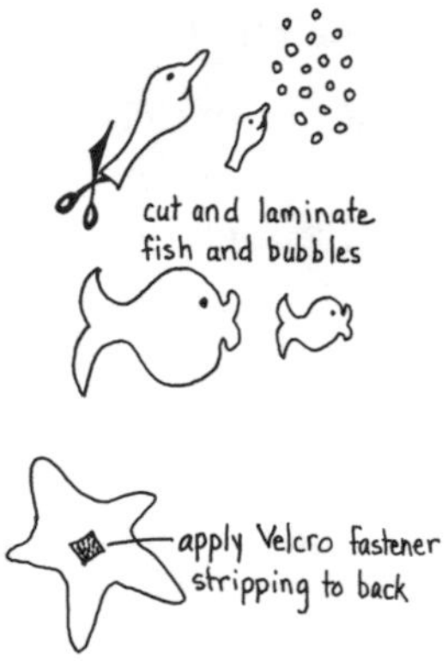

3. With the poster board, make one small fish and one large fish of each type (starfish, sea horse, jellyfish, kissing fish, swordfish, and sunfish). Cut them out, laminate them, and glue the hooked fasteners to the back of each fish. For an easier activity, make each pair of fish a different color (possibly the primary and secondary colors). If you want the board to be difficult, make all types of fish the same color.

figure #2

cut and laminate fish and bubbles

apply Velcro fastener stripping to back

4. Cut out bubbles from blue poster board, laminate them, and glue hooked fasteners to the backs.

5. Cut a strip of sandpaper the length of the bottom of the bulletin board. Pin or staple to the bottom of the bowl shape.

6. Cut seaweed shapes out of green felt and pin or staple them onto the bulletin board.

7. Position the fish at random in the bowl on the board.

There are several different activities you can do with this board. Move the fish around on the board making sets of matching types of fish. Make sets of all of the small and large fish. Use the bulletin board fish bowl to tell stories, sing songs, or recite finger plays. If you have a looped fabric cube with the numerals 1 to 6 on it, roll it and put that many fish in the bowl or that many bubbles coming out of a fish's mouth. Encourage children to use their imaginations for manipulating the board in a variety of ways.

Flannel, Magnetic, and Looped Fabric Board

Make a board that works with all three of the above materials.

You will need:

* ★ a piece of plywood or similar material about 2' x 3' and 1/2" thick

* ★ a piece of sheet metal about 2" smaller than the wood

* ★ a piece of flannel fabric about 1" larger than the wood; a neutral color is best

* ★ a piece of looped fabric the same size as the flannel fabric

* ★ staple gun and staples

* ★ sewing machine, needle and heavy-duty thread

* ★ duct tape

* ★ optional: a picture frame the size of the wood

1. Staple the sheet of metal to the plywood with the staple gun. Apply duct tape around the edges of the metal to secure it and assure there will be no sharp edges.

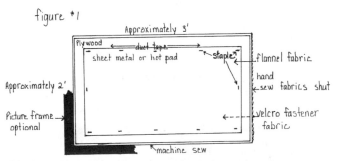

2. Machine sew your piece of flannel and piece of looped fabric together, right sides together, along three sides of the rectangle. Turn right side out.

3. Slip the fabric onto the board so the flannel is covering the sheet metal.

4. On the open end of the fabric, with the raw edges, turn edges in. Hand sew it with an overcast stitch so it is tight on the board.

5. Optional: Place your board in a picture frame to finish off your raw edges.

On the side that has the sheet metal and flannel you can use magnetic pieces and/or felt pieces. On the looped fabric side, you can use any type of material (poster board, foam rubber place mat, or stiff pellon), providing that you have a small strip of the hooked fastener on the back of the piece.

Looped Fabric Covered Barrel

A looped fabric barrel is unusual but also practical. You can also use the barrel for storage.

You will need:

* ★ a large cardboard barrel about 3' high and 1-1/2' in diameter (you can purchase these for a small price from factories that store spices, dry soup mixtures, etc.)

* ★ 2 yards of looped fabric

* ★ craft glue

* ★ scissors

* ★ small screw driver

* ★ heavy-duty curved needle and thread, hot glue gun, or quick bonding glue

* ★ optional: cording

1. Clean out the inside of the barrel.

2. Cut the looped fabric the same length of the barrel and large enough so it wraps completely around the barrel (it may need to be pieced together if the fabric doesn't fit the barrel's dimensions).

3. Many barrels have a metal rim around the top and the bottom. Tuck your looped fabric into the metal rim, securing with craft glue as you go around. A small screwdriver can help you push the fabric under the metal, providing a finished edge

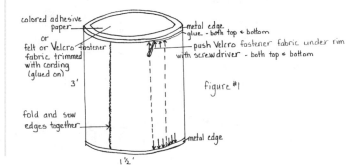

around the top and bottom. To assure it will be even, tuck and glue a couple of inches at the top and then a couple of inches at the bottom, repeating until you are all the way around the barrel.

4. After you have glued and tucked all the way around the barrel, you will have an open seam the length of the barrel. Sew the raw edges together with a heavy-duty curved needle and thread. A hot glue gun or quick bonding glue are options for this step.

Make use of the lid if one is available. Some lids are metal. If that is the case, cut a circular piece of colored contact paper and apply it to the surface of the lid. Now you have a round and decorative magnetic board. If your lid is cardboard like the barrel, cut a circular piece of felt or looped fabric and hot glue it to the lid. You have a portable felt board or another looped fabric board. Cording, hot glued around the edge of the fabric, will finish off the raw edges.

Handmade Puzzles

You can make puzzles in many ways—from simple to complex. The puzzle described below is durable and easy to make. You would probably not leave these puzzles out all of the time. Pull them out for special times of the day (magic carpet activities) or when they tie into a particular theme.

You will need:

* ★ heavy-duty poster board
* ★ rubber cement
* ★ a picture for the face of the puzzle; such as a picture the children have colored or painted, posters or wall decorations from card shops, or pictures from old calendars
* ★ clear contact paper
* ★ sharp scissors or paper cutter
* ★ permanent marker
* ★ reclosable plastic bag
* ★ optional: iron and ironing board, scrap cloth, stick pin

1. Cut the poster board to about the size of

figure #1

back of picture

posterboard

rubber cement complete areas and let dry thoroughly

the picture. Apply rubber cement on the complete back of one picture and one complete side of the poster board. Let the cement dry thoroughly.

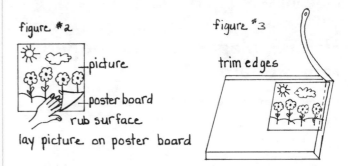

figure #2

picture

poster board

rub surface

lay picture on poster board

figure #3

trim edges

2. When the cement has dried on both pieces, carefully lay the picture face up on the poster board. Note: Once you have made contact with the picture and the poster board they will not come apart. Be sure you have it positioned the way you want it. Rub over the complete surface so all corners are securely cemented to the poster board.

3. If necessary, trim the edges of your poster board/picture with scissors or paper cutter.

4. Cover both the front and back of the poster board/picture with clear contact

figure #4

rub surface

cover both sides with clear adhesive paper

trim edges

paper. Rub the surface to remove any bubbles and get a thorough contact. Trim the edges of the contact paper.

5. Optional: Iron your puzzle to make sure the contact paper has bonded and to eliminate cloudiness. The iron should be dry (not steam) and set at about medium heat. Lay your puzzle on the ironing board and cover it with a scrap cloth (old cotton bed sheets are a good thickness). Keeping the iron moving, iron over the complete surface of the puzzle, both front and back. Check the puzzle after about thirty seconds to see if it looks like you have ironed over the complete surface. If you have created bubbles with the heat of the iron, do not rub them. Let them return to the surface by themselves. If they aren't disappearing, prick them with the stick pin, which will let the air out of them. This method is also helpful if wrinkles have formed in the contact paper.

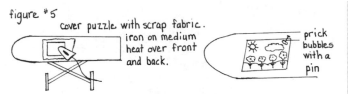

figure #5
cover puzzle with scrap fabric. iron on medium heat over front and back.

prick bubbles with a pin

6. Using sharp scissors or paper cutter, cut your puzzle into the desired amount of pieces. For young preschoolers, consider three or four pieces and so on up to ten to fifteen pieces as their abilities develop. As you cut, make your splits in places easy for children to distinguish the placement (through the face of a person, or through the middle of an animal's body).

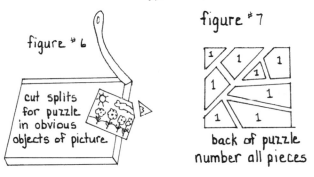

figure #6

cut splits for puzzle in obvious objects of picture.

figure #7

back of puzzle number all pieces

7. If you have made several puzzles, number the backs of the pieces with permanent marker. For the first puzzle, draw a 1 on all of the pieces of that puzzle; for the second puzzle, put a 2 on all of the pieces, and so on. Numbering the pieces makes sorting easy if the puzzles get mixed together.

8. Store your puzzles in plastic reclosable bags.

Individual Felt Box

Individual felt boxes are great for storing individual felt pieces—the felt board is on the inside lid of the school box. A felt box is a good way to help children learn some organizational skills. Pieces are available to the children without you needing to take time to pass them out.

You will need:

* enough cardboard school boxes for each child in your group (cigar or shoe boxes work well and are a free alternative)

* felt squares

* scissors

* craft glue or hot glue gun

* felt pieces

* optional: colored or printed contact paper, looped fabric, decorative boxes with lids

1. Cut the felt slightly smaller than the inside lid of the box (so the lid still shuts completely). Make sure you cut straight edges.

2. Glue the edges of the felt piece to the inside of the lid. Children can open their box and use the lid for a felt board.

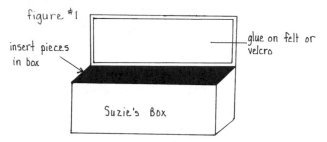

figure #1

insert pieces in box

glue on felt or velcro

Suzie's Box

3. Place the individual felt pieces in the box so they are easily accessible to the children.

Use looped fabric as an alternative to felt. If you use cigar or shoe boxes, cover with colored or printed contact paper.

Handmade Photo Books

Handmade books are inexpensive items that bring hours of joy and interest to children. One of the many advantages of these books is the ease in changing and updating them as new events and activities occur. All you need to do is add new pages. Place your book on the shelf or in the box with the rest of the books and let the children enjoy it.

You will need:

* several sheets of white or colored poster board

* several gallon size reclosable plastic bags

* two 1″ to 2″ metal book rings

* colored, solid, and/or printed contact paper

* scissors

* paper punch

* markers

* ruler

* rubber cement

★ photographs or pictures drawn by the children

★ optional: permanent markers, vinyl letters

1. Cut four 11″ x 12″ pieces of poster board. Double these sheets and use them for the front and back covers.

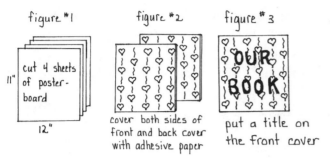

figure #1

11″ — cut 4 sheets of poster-board — 12″

figure #2

cover both sides of front and back cover with adhesive paper

figure #3

OUR BOOK

put a title on the front cover

2. Cover the doubled pieces of poster board with colored, solid, and/or printed contact paper.

3. Title your book on the front cover. It could be as simple as "Our Book" or "(Child's name) Book." Either print it on with permanent markers or cut letters from a contrasting color of contact paper. Another option is to purchase vinyl letters and adhere them to the cover.

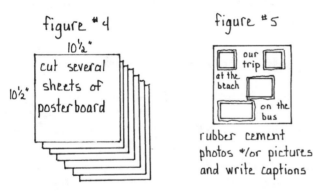

figure #4

10½″

10½″ — cut several sheets of posterboard

figure #5

our trip / at the beach / on the bus

rubber cement photos ★/or pictures and write captions

4. Cut several pieces of poster board into 10-1/2″ squares. Two will be placed back sides together and inserted into the reclosable plastic bags. The number of sheets you cut will be determined by the amount of photographs or pages you want in your book.

5. Mount pictures with rubber cement on the pieces of poster board. Add captions and dates by the pictures.

6. Insert each finished page sideways into a reclosable bag and zip it shut.

figure #6

our trip / at the beach / on the bus

insert pages and zip baggie shut

7. Punch two holes in both covers along the left side about 5″ apart and about 1/2″ from the edge. Make sure your holes are positioned and punched evenly on both the front and back covers. Line pages up evenly inside the book and punch holes in them along the flaps of plastic, above the zip shut strip. These should also be punched evenly—about 5″ apart and 3/8″ from the edge.

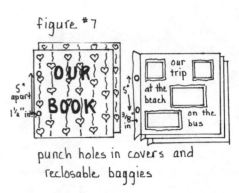

figure #7

OUR BOOK

5″ apart / 1½″ in / 5″ / 3/8″ in

our trip / at the beach / on the bus

punch holes in covers and reclosable baggies

8. Use metal book rings to join the covers and pages. Now your handmade book will open up from the side similar to a regular book.

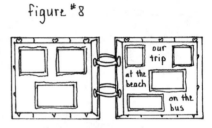

figure #8

our trip / at the beach / on the bus

Attach pages and covers with rings.

Circle of Match-Ups

Circle of match-ups is a game made on a circular piece of poster board. It is self-correcting by using aluminum foil and a continuity tester. When children make a correct match, the continuity tester lights up because it completes an electrical circuit. Choose matching objects of any topic or concept you want to reinforce. Make several games and include them in your magic carpet activities collection. Consider the developmental abilities of your group. Make some of your circle match-ups simple and others more complex. The possibilities are endless.

You will need:

★ poster board

★ stickers, rubber stamp and ink pad, or stencils

★ aluminum foil

★ masking tape

* paper punch

* scissors

* clear and/or colored contact paper

* continuity tester; at hardware or auto parts stores for $3 to $15 (choose one that has a blunt or rounded end or sand down the sharp point). Closely supervise children who use continuity testers and discuss their use before anyone uses them.

1. Cut a circle out of poster board about 12″ in diameter.

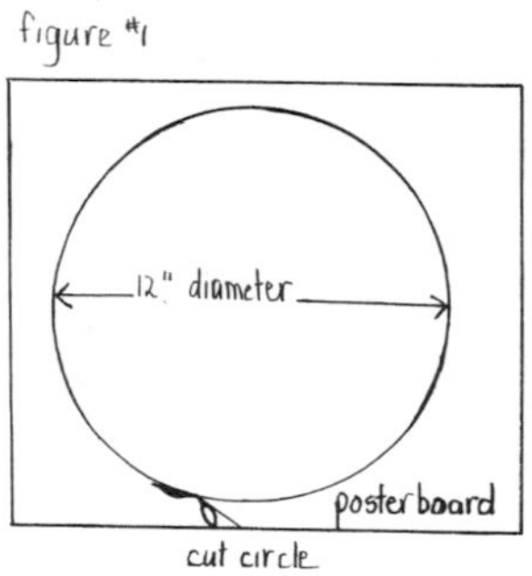

figure #1

12″ diameter

poster board

cut circle

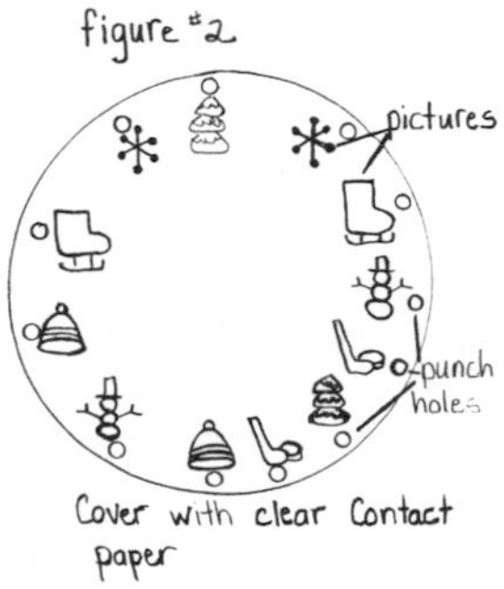

figure #2

pictures

punch holes

Cover with clear Contact paper

2. Position your stickers, rubber stamps, or stencils (two of each design) about 1″ apart and 1 1/2″ in from the edge, around the complete circle.

3. Cover front of circle with clear contact paper.

4. Punch a hole with a paper punch, between the edge of the circle and each picture.

5. Tear about 3″ of aluminum foil off of the roll and fold it several times making a 1/2″ wide strip.

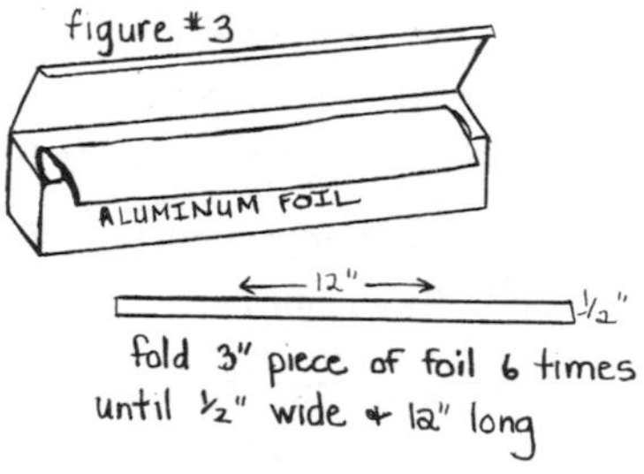

figure #3

ALUMINUM FOIL

12″

1/2″

fold 3″ piece of foil 6 times until 1/2″ wide + 12″ long

6. Lay one strip of aluminum foil across the back of the circle, from one paper punch to the other, connecting a pair of matching pictures. Tape the aluminum foil down with masking tape. Cover the complete strip of aluminum foil with tape so you don't get double connections with the continuity tester. Also, make sure that

figure #4

tape
foil
punch

aluminum foil is showing under each punch hole because this is what is going to make your continuity tester light up.

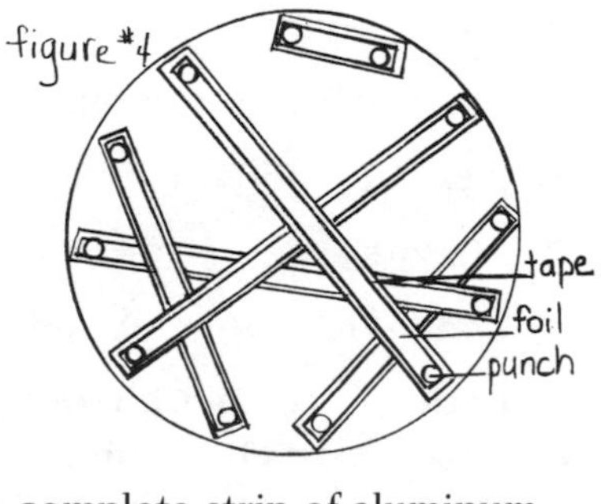

7. Continue steps 5 and 6 until you have connected each match with aluminum foil, taping every time.

8. Cover the back of the circle with clear or colored contact paper.

figure #5

Cover back with clear or colored Contact paper

Test your game with the continuity tester to make sure it is working and that you made the right matches with the aluminum foil.

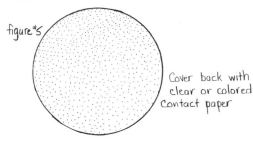

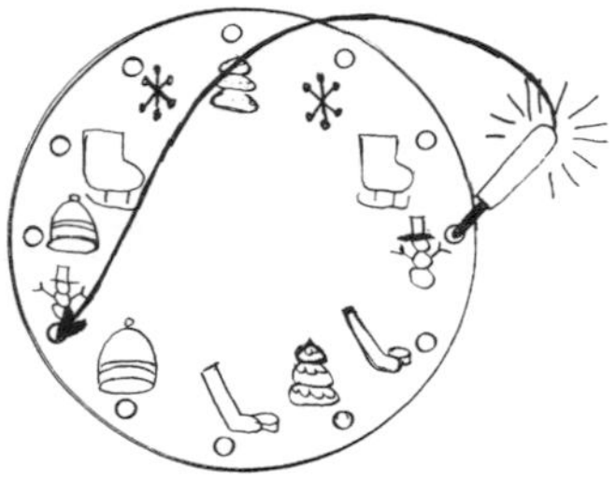

Buddy Buckets

You will need:

* a 5-quart ice cream bucket or a round plastic basket about the same size

* 1 yard of brightly colored or patterned fabric

* 3 yards of 1/2″ white cording

* sewing machine; or craft glue or hot glue gun

* clear or patterned contact paper

* scissors

* ruler

* optional: hand punch

1. Take the yard of fabric and cut off 12″.

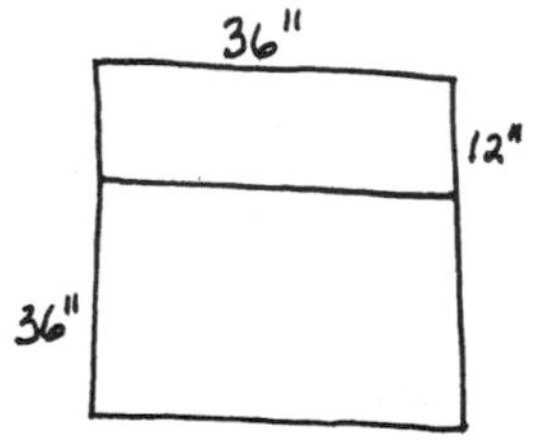

36″

12″

36″

2. Sew or glue the two ends together to form a circle. Put a 1″ hem on open edges.

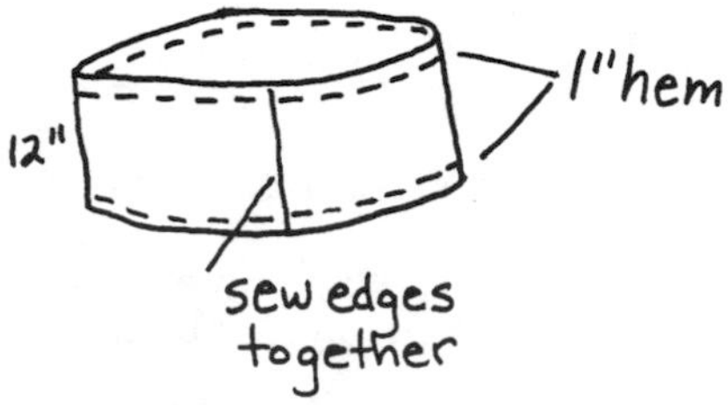

1″ hem

12″

sew edges together

3. Make button holes or cut slits at 3″ intervals on one hemmed edge, insert 24″ cording through the other hemmed edge.

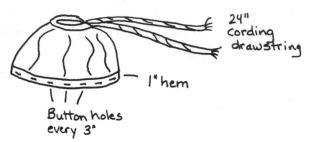

4. Decorate the bucket with colored or patterned contact paper.

5. Punch holes around the top of the ice cream bucket at 2″ or 3″ intervals. The basket should have open holes already to use.

6. With 1-1/2 yards of cording, lace the fabric piece to the bucket or basket, going through the holes of the fabric and bucket.

Dog and Bones Game

You will need:

* dry doggie treats that come in variety of shapes
* poster board 12″ x 24″
* small plastic dish
* markers
* reclosable plastic bags
* clear contact paper
* scissors
* ruler
* optional: laminating machine

1. Measure and rule off 2″ x 2″ squares (fifty of them) on the poster board.

2. Using a colored marker, trace ten of each shaped doggie treat in the squares. Use a different color

marker for each shape. Write numbers that children are familiar with inside the treat shapes.

3. Cover with contact paper or laminate. Cut into squares.

4. Prepare the doggie figure (see full size pattern on page 115).

5. Place the doggie treats in the reclosable plastic bag.

The directions for the game: Place the dog on the edge of the plastic dish. Turn the shape-number cards upside down. Place the doggie treats in a pile on the floor. Children take turns drawing the shape-number cards. The child matches the treat shape and counts the number of treats to put in the doggie's dish. Children continue to take turns until all the treats have been fed to the dog. Children can help each other with counting if needed.

Magnetic Wands, Objects, and Paths

You will need:

* circular magnet (about 1″ in diameter); purchased in craft stores
* tongue depressor; purchased in drug stores
* objects to magnetize, for example decorative erasers, pom-pom pal (page 102), or Styrofoam packing pieces made into an object
* metal tacks or small circular magnets (about 1/2″ in diameter)
* miscellaneous items such as feathers, pipe cleaners, garland, etc.
* poster board
* water based and permanent markers
* clear or colored contact paper
* scissors
* craft glue or quick bonding glue
* optional: magnetic wand (used to take up magnetic bingo chips, pins, or for science experiments) purchased in discount, fabric, or educational stores

For Handmade Magnetic Wand

1. Glue the magnet to the end of a tongue depressor. Use craft glue or quick bonding glue to assure its security. Note: purchased magnetic wands work equally as well and are inexpensive.

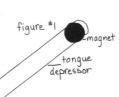

figure #1

magnet

tongue depressor

For Magnetic Objects

2. Either you or the children create a magnetic object. Some possibilities are listed below:

* A purchased decorative eraser in various shapes such as animals, shoes, or cartoon characters. Use as three-dimensional objects. Glue the smaller magnet to the base of the eraser or push the tack into the base.

figure #2

squeeze quick bonding glue on tack and push into eraser or glue magnet to bottom of eraser

* Pom-pom pals make a great magnetic object. Glue several pom-poms together with craft glue to create a new creature. Glue the smaller magnet to the base of the pom-pom or push the tack into the base.

magnet or tack

* Decorate Styrofoam packing pieces with materials such as pipe cleaners, feathers, and garlands. Glue Styrofoam pieces

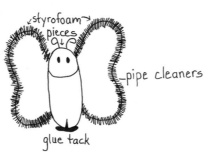

styrofoam pieces

pipe cleaners

glue tack

together and items on it to create creatures such as crocodiles, butterflies, or robots. Coloring with permanent markers is a possibility, also. Finish off by gluing the smaller magnet to the base of the Styrofoam ball or push the tack into the base.

* With water based markers, draw pictures on poster board. Cut out the pictures and cover with clear contact paper. Glue the smaller magnet on the back.

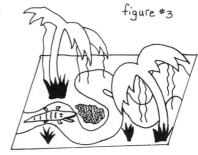

thread whiskers

yarn

tail

poster board with magnet glued under

Note: Objects that have steady, flat bottoms and ones that are lightweight, such as pom-pom pals and creatures, work fine with tacks. Other objects that are a little heavier and not as flat on the bottom, such as erasers, work best with the smaller circular 1/2" magnet.

For Poster Board Path

3. Draw a path on a piece of poster board (about 10" x 10"). Make as simple or complex as you desire.

* An example for a crocodile magnetic object would be a jungle scene that it can swim and walk through. Make three-dimensional

figure #3

trees and bushes out of poster board or other materials for the crocodile to move around.

* A simpler path is a curved and twisted line with a start and a finish point for the object to follow.

Finish

Start

Note: Cover poster board path with clear contact paper. Magnets will still work and the path will stay clean and durable. Another option is to cover the poster board with colored contact paper and draw your path on with permanent markers.

Place your wand, magnetic object, and path in a reclosable gallon size plastic bag and put it on your magic carpet activity shelf. If you have three-dimensional paths, put your items in a box for storage.

Storytelling Mitten

Create this versatile mitten and use with pom-pom pals page 102.

You will need:

* two 12" square pieces of looped fabric material

* hooked fastener strips

* pen or pencil

* sewing machine or needle and thread

* scissors

1. Using your hand as a pattern, draw a mitten shape on the back side of the looped fabric material. Make the shape about 2" larger than your hand shape. Cut out two pieces.

2. Hand or machine sew the two pieces together along the rounded edges, right sides together. Leave a 1/2" seam allowance. Do not sew along the straight, or wrist, edge. Turn the mitten right side out.

3. Attach a hooked fastener to the bottom of a pom-pom pal. The surface of the looped fabric will accept the fastener.

Ribbons and Rings

You will need:

* colored plastic party favor bracelets

* 2 yards of 1/4" satin ribbon in colors to match each bracelet

* scissors

* ruler

1. Cut ribbons into 1-yard lengths.

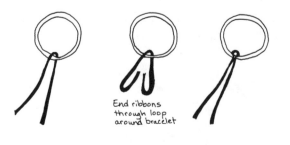

End ribbons through loop around bracelet

2. Attach 1 yard of ribbon to the matching colored bracelet.

3. Attach every color of ribbon to the teacher's bracelet.

Peek Hole Folders

Peek hole folders are regular file folders with magazine photos inside them; they are durable and easy to store. Search for photos of interest to children and compile a large collection of these guessing games. Rotate to keep children's interest level high.

You will need:

* **several folders; colored ones are eye-appealing**

* **several magazine photos or old calendar pictures**

* **rubber cement**

* **pointed scissors**

* **optional: a variety of poems, lamination**

1. Choose a large magazine photo, about 8" x 10". Trim the edges so they are smooth and straight.

2. Apply rubber cement to the entire back of the photo and the right, inside flap of the folder. Let them dry completely.

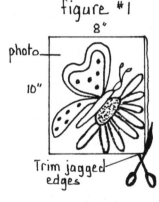

figure #1
8"
photo
10"
Trim jagged edges

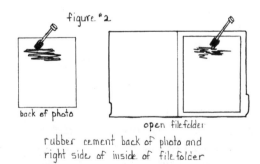

figure #2
back of photo
open file folder
rubber cement back of photo and right side of inside of file folder

3. When they are dry, carefully lay the photo onto the cemented flap of the folder and rub off excess rubber cement around the edges. Note: Once they are stuck together, they will not come apart.

4. Lay the top flap of the folder on the picture and estimate the best spots for peek hole. Once you have determined where the holes should go, lift the flap and cut a hole about 1/2" to 1" in diameter.

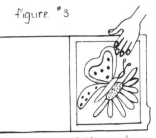

figure #3

lay photo on folder and rub excess rubber cement off

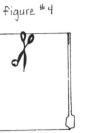

figure #4

cut peek hole ½"-1" diameter

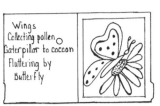

figure #5

Wings
Collecting pollen
Caterpillar to cocoon
Fluttering by
Butterfly

5. Optional: Find a poem that goes with the picture and print it on the left inside flap of the folder. Although this is optional, using a poem with the picture is a good way to introduce poetry and facts of the photo.

6. To make the peek hole folder extra durable, laminate it. Once it is laminated, recut the peek hole so you can see through it.

Pattern for Dog and Bones Game, page 112

"Hello" in Several Languages

Hello!

Spanish—Buenos Dias (Bway-nohs Dee ahs) or Hola (Oh-la)

Russian—Privet (Pri-vit)

Chinese—Wei (Wee)

German—Guten Tag (Goot-n Tahk)

Hebrew—Shalom (Shah lohm)

Hawaiian—Aloha (Ah-LOH-hah)

Swahili—Jambo (Jahm-boh)

French—Bonjour (Bohn-zhoor) or Salut (Sah-loo)

Japanese—Konnichi Wa (Kon-ni-chi Wah)

Dutch—Hallo (Hah-loh)

Italian—Ciao (Chow)

Hmong—Nyob Zoo (Nyah Zhong)

English—Hello, Hi, or Howdy

Note: The phonetic spellings in parentheses are our own which should help you pronounce these greetings with ease.

Sign Language—

Hello

or

Hi

"Hello, Hello" in Three Languages

Hmong

Nyob zoo, nyob zoo, nyob zoo, (Nyaw zhong, nyaw zhong, nyaw zhong): Hello, hello, hello,

Thiab kob nyob li cas lawn? (Tee-ah caw nyaw lee kee-ya lah): And how are you?

Kuv nyob zoo, (Goo nyaw zhong): I'm fine, I'm fine,

Thiab kuv xav tias koj nyob zoo thiab. (Tee-ah goo sah thee-ah caw nyaw zhong tee-ah): And I hope that you are, too.

(These are phonetically spelled.)

Spanish

Hola, hola, hola, (Oh-la, oh-la, oh-la): Hello, hello, hello,

Y como estas tu? (E co-mow es-ta too): And how are you?

Yo bien, yo bien, (Yo bee-en, yo bee-en) I'm fine, I'm fine,

Y espero tu tambien. (E es-pear-o too tom-bee-en): And I hope that you are, too.

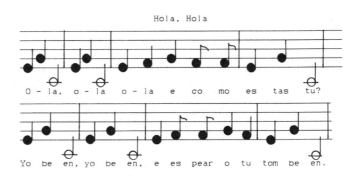

French

Bonjour, bonjour, bonjour, (Bohn-zhoor, bohn-zhoor, bohn-zhoor): Hello, hello, hello,

Et comment allez-vous? (Ah co-ma ta-lay-vu): And how are you?

Je suis bien, je suis bien, (Jay swee bee-en, jay swee bee-en): I'm fine, I'm fine,

Et j'espere que vous etes aussi. (Ah je-spare kuh vuz-et oh-see): And I hope that you are, too.

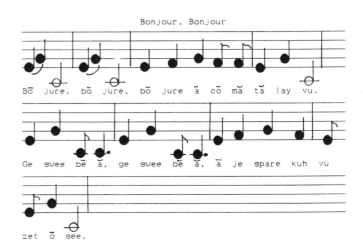

Appendix

D

Forms for Evaluation and Reflection

Setting the Stage

The following activity will help you pinpoint areas of the classroom where the most frequent disputes or disruptions occur.

Room Arrangement Observation

In the space below, draw a simple floor plan of your classroom. Include all interest areas, equipment, and furniture. Show everything, including bathrooms, cubby areas, windows, and doors.

Post your floor plan in a convenient location in your room for one week. On the floor plan, indicate with an X the areas where any disruptions occur. A disruption is an incident that children cannot resolve on their own and a teacher needs to assist them. Color code the X's to indicate disruptions that happened in the morning and ones that happened in the afternoon.

Make a photocopy of the page for observation purposes.

Reflection

After a week, look at your floor plan and identify problem areas. Then review the classroom evaluation scale in part 1, chapter 1. Look at each category (selecting materials, developmental appropriateness, accessibility/storage, etc.). List any problems from columns 1 or 3 that are contributing to problem areas identified in your classroom.

Changes I need to make:

_____
_____
_____
_____
_____
_____
_____
_____
_____
_____
_____
_____
_____
_____
_____
_____
_____
_____
_____
_____
_____
_____
_____

Juggling Your Day

The following activity will help you examine your present schedule. When completed, this observation will indicate which times of the day are most difficult for your group.

My Daily Schedule Observation

Write your daily schedule in the space below. Post your schedule in a convenient location in your room for one week. Indicate with an X any time during the day when children's behavior is particularly chaotic or disruptive and/or requires teacher assistance. You may want to use a different color for each day.

My Daily Schedule

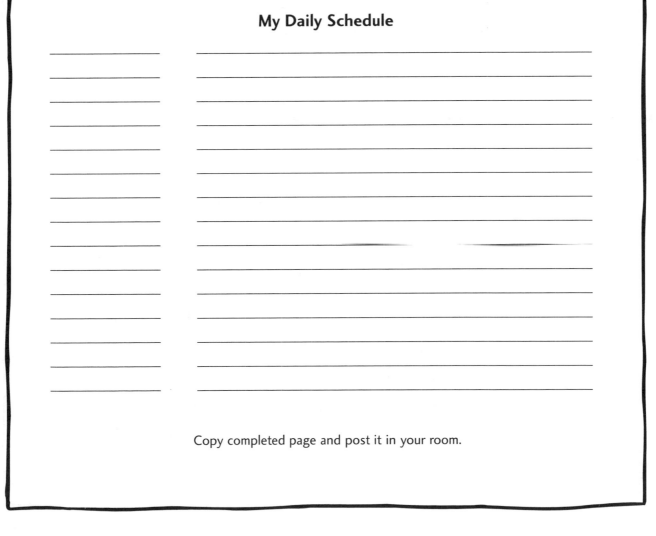

Copy completed page and post it in your room.

© 1994 *Transition Magician*, Redleaf Press, 450 North Syndicate, Suite 5, St. Paul, MN 55104, 1-800-423-8309

Reflection

After a week's observation, identify the problem times in your schedule. Ask yourself these questions and circle your answer. (If you do not wish to write in this book, photocopy this page to use for your evaluation.)

1. Did I find trouble spots in my schedule?   YES   NO

2. Where are my trouble spots? Which routine is most difficult?

   _____

   _____

   _____

   _____

3. What is causing the trouble? (Is it length of the activity, lack of active involvement of children, etc.?)

   _____

   _____

   _____

   _____

4. Are my expectations clear?   YES   NO

5. Do I explain the transition, give children a warning, etc.? YES   NO

6. Are there too many transitions?   YES   NO

7. Are waiting times during transitions too long?   YES   NO

8. Is there enough adult supervision?   YES   NO

9. Are problems due to poor planning?   YES   NO

10. Were you able to pinpoint your trouble spots?   YES   NO

My Plan of Action

Make a plan to change your room arrangement or schedule. Review your plan after two weeks. (If you do not wish to write in this book, you may photocopy this page.)

Goal 1

_____

Action Steps:

_____

_____

_____

Goal 2

_____

Action Steps:

_____

_____

_____

Goal 3

_____

Action Steps:

_____

_____

_____

Glossary

Attention Grabbers—Interesting objects or brief activities designed to get and focus children's attention. For greatest attention getting results, present children with a little suspense, surprise, or mystery.

Bag of Tricks—Collection of amusing and quick-to-use learning opportunities to facilitate transitions with children.

Classroom Setting—The general term used for the environment in variety of early childhood programs.

Concepts—A basic fact or idea, such as numbers, colors, and shapes.

Contact Paper—Self-adhesive decorative covering; available in clear, colored, or patterned.

Cooperative Learning—A group of children working towards a common goal.

Cubbies—Individual shelf and hanging space for children's personal belongings.

Curriculum Theme—The topic or focus for learning determined by the teacher's plans and the children's interests.

Daily Schedule—The order and length of time of activities and routines throughout the day.

Developmental Areas—A term used to collectively describe skills in the cognitive, social/emotional, physical/motor, communication/language, and self-help areas of a classroom setting.

Developmentally Appropriate Practice (DAP)—A position paper published by The National Association for the Education of Young Children (NAEYC) that provides guidelines for developmentally appropriate programs for children from birth through eight years of age.

Dramatic Play—Children taking on roles of people and animals and interacting in various play situations, such as a hospital, store, or office.

Early Childhood Education (ECE)—Programs for children ages three through five years, including but not limited to special education classes, Chapter I classes, kindergartens, four-year-olds kindergartens.

Extenders (or Expanders)—Activities that extend or expand children's knowledge about current themes or previously learned topics.

Family Living Center—A dramatic play setting that imitates home situations. Also known as the housekeeping or doll corner.

Finger Plays—Simple rhymes, spoken or sung, and dramatized by finger and hand motions.

Free Choice—The portion of the day when children are able to choose from activities provided and make decisions about their active participation.

Gatherings—Children and teacher(s) together for a specific purpose.

Guidance—Leading, directing, and training children with the goal of developing self-control.

Laminate—The process of covering a paper or printed material with thin sheets of clear plastic. The thin sheets of plastic are applied by a machine using heat.

Learning Centers—Activity areas set up in an early childhood setting that respond to the interests and developmental needs of the children.

Looped Fabric—Various fabrics including headliner and tempo.

Magical Moments—Times when a group of children are between activities, on the move, or out of the room. Creative use of the environment and small portable materials provide opportunities that occupy children in a productive manner.

Magic Carpet Activities—Learning activities used in a special place. Many are self-correcting activities used individually. Others are cooperative in nature and used by pairs of children.

Magnetic Board—Metal surface prepared to attract magnetic pieces.

National Association for the Education of Young Children (NAEYC)—An organization for professionals working with young children.

Olfactory—Relating to or connected with the sense of smell.

Pellon—Stiff felt found in fabric stores. Also known as pennant material.

Push Button Music Boxes—Small inexpensive music disc activated by pushing the side or button.

Resource Person—A person who has a skill, talent, or particular profession or vocation and shares knowledge with others.

Rhythm Sticks—Pairs of finished wooden sticks (made from dowels) used to tap out rhythms and patterns of movement.

Routine—A procedure within a daily schedule that is regularly followed. In a child care setting, typical routine activities are arrival, breakfast, snack, lunch, hand washing, toileting, nap or rest time, and departure.

Sensory Cue—A signal that indicates a change in routines or activities. A cue can be auditory, visual, olfactory or tactile or a combination. A cue often accompanies a verbal direction.

Settlers—Techniques used to gather children together and prepare and quiet them for the upcoming group time.

Sit-Upons—Cushion or pad, either handmade or bought.

Stretchers—Exercises that get children and staff moving and stretching. Often needed for a change of pace or to break up intense concentration.

Tactile—Relating to the sense of touch.

Transition—The movement of children from one activity or routine to another during the day. The transition becomes an activity itself if planned and facilitated.

Triple A—Anticipate, Act, and Avert. A strategy for teachers to guide children's behavior. First, anticipate times and situations that children will need teacher guidance. Second, act by making changes in the environment or using transitional activities. Anticipating and acting help to avert behavior problems and ease the transition.

Velcro—A brand name for looped fabric and hooked fastener materials, available by the yard with adhesive or sew-on backings.

Vignette—A short descriptive story. The stories in this book illustrate situations that teachers often encounter.

Visual Aids—Tangibles and props used to accompany teacher instruction.

Wait Time—The time children have to wait while their classmates finish an activity or routine; the time before another activity or routine begins.

You're Excused—The method used to dismiss children from a group activity and transition them to another activity.

References

Alger, Harriet A. "Transitions: Alternatives to Manipulative Management Techniques." *Young Children*. Washington, DC: NAEYC (September 1984).

Baker, Betty R. "Transition Time: Make It a Time of Learning for Children." *Day Care and Early Education* (Summer 1986).

Bredekamp, S., ed. *Developmentally Appropriate Practice in Early Childhood Programs Serving Children from Birth through Age 8*. Washington, DC: National Association for the Education of Young Children, 1987.

Hawley, W., and S. Rosenholtz. "Good Schools: What Research Says about Improving Student Achievement." *Peabody Journal of Education* 61, No.4, (Summer, 1984).

Mitchell, G. *A Very Practical Guide to Discipline*. Chelsea, MA: Telshare Publishing Co., 1982.

Saifer, Steffen. *Practical Solutions to Practically Every Problem*. St. Paul, MN: Redleaf Press, 1990.

Stallings, J. "Allocated Academic Learning Time Revisited, or Beyond Time on Task." *Educational Researcher* 9(1980).

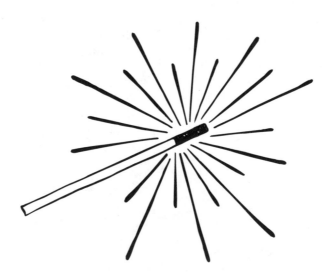